Stanley and Munro Price

—

THE ROAD
TO APOCALYPSE

—

The Extraordinary Journey of Lewis Way

Notting Hill Editions

Published in 2011
by Notting Hill Editions Ltd
Newcombe House, 45 Notting Hill Gate
London W11 3LQ

Designed by FLOK Design, Berlin, Germany
Typeset by CB editions, London

Printed and bound
by Memminger MedienCentrum, Memmingen, Germany

A CIP record for this book
is available from the British Library
ISBN 978-1-90790326-7

www.nottinghilleditions.com

To Judy – referee

– Acknowledgements –

We would like to thank Lieutenant-Colonel Jeremy Metcalfe, OBE, for his kind help and cooperation in giving us access to the papers and pictures of his forebear Lewis Way. Mrs Mary David and Anne David were also most helpful in letting us see Lewis Way's Tracts and the story books and drawings of the Way children on their Grand Tour. We very much appreciated the help and cooperation of Dr C. M. Woolgar, Head of Special Collections at the Hartley Library at University of Southampton, Julia Walworth, Fellow Librarian of Merton College, Oxford, Sue Stafford of the Gloucester Genealogical Society, Roger Bettridge, Buckinghamshire County Archivist, our fine editor Lucasta Miller, and Simon Cox and his camera.

For Zion's sake,
I will not rest.
I will not hold my peace,
Until Jerusalem be blessed
And Judah dwell at ease.

Hymn written by Lewis Way
(after Isaiah LXII)

Lewis Way painted by James Leakey on the eve
of his journey to Russia, 1817

Contents

– Introduction –

For more than sixty years, Israel and its conflicts with its neighbours have formed one of the world's most intractable problems. When the state was founded in 1948, the aim of the Zionist movement was fulfilled. A homeland for the Jewish people had finally been secured, but it was never to 'dwell at ease'. Since its inception the state has either been at war with its Arab neighbours or defending itself against terrorist groups or freedom fighters, a description dependent on what side you take. The ideals of Zionism have become contentious even in Israel itself, not just between Arab and Jew, but between Right and Left, secular and religious, conflicts which are reflected in the Diaspora, which has 8.3 million Jews to Israel's 5 million.

Yet the original ideology of Zionism, with its call for an independent Jewish state in Palestine, was simple and straightforward. It was a late-nineteenth-century nationalist movement, made urgent by outbreaks of resurgent anti-Semitism across Europe. The pogroms and persecutions in the 1880s in Russia led to a huge wave of Jewish emigration westward, mostly to America. But the dramatic moment of Zionism's birth was in Paris on 18 January 1895. Theodor Herzl, a Viennese journalist and playwright, was pressed against the railings of the Ecole Militaire listening to the anti-Semitic shouts of the crowd as they watched Alfred Dreyfus, a Jewish officer in the French army, being publicly humiliated after a false accusation of treason. Dreyfus was to spend four years on Devil's Island before being re-tried and eventually exonerated. In that time Herzl had written *Der Judenstaat*, gained international attention for the idea of a Jewish state in Palestine and held the first Zionist Congress in Basel. Herzl then proceeded personally to plead the Zionist cause with world leaders, the Czar, the Kaiser and the Sultan. He received offers of land for the Jewish people from the Sultan – Mesopotamia (if they paid off the Turkish National Debt); and from the British Colonial Secretary – El Arish in Egypt; the offer was later changed to Uganda. Herzl and the Zionists refused anything but Palestine. Exhausted by his work, Herzl died at the age of forty-four and was accorded virtually a state funeral in Vienna.

With the idea of a Jewish homeland at least established, the progress of political Zionism continued. As Herzl had realised, this could only be achieved with the backing of a great power. In the closing years of World War I, it was the British who became the inheritors of this historic burden. Chaim Weizmann, Herzl's successor, had gained the ear of

Arthur Balfour, the British foreign minister, and persuaded him of the righteousness of the Zionist cause. In his turn Balfour persuaded the prime minister, Lloyd George, and in November 1917 the British government issued the Balfour Declaration which gave its slightly ambiguous promise of 'the establishment in Palestine of a national home for the Jewish people'. In 1918, at the head of a British army which had defeated the Turks, General Allenby marched into Jerusalem. In the wake of the war, the Ottoman empire was finally divided up and Britain given the Mandate for Palestine. It was to take another thirty years, another World War and a Holocaust for a 'national home' to become an independent state.

If the backing of one great power in the form of Britain was essential to the establishment of the Jewish homeland, the support of another, the United States, has remained crucial to its survival ever since. After thirty stormy years of administering the Mandate, the British were more than happy to get rid of it. America then became the protector of the new State of Israel for a variety of reasons – humanitarian sympathy for the Jews after the Holocaust, support for a strategically placed ally during the Cold War, and most recently the dictates of the War on Terror. Yet alongside these diplomatic and military motivations stood an important religious factor – not Jewish, but Christian Zionism.

Christian Zionism has been a core belief of millions of Americans since the late nineteenth century. Its political influence, however, dates from the late 1970s, when the television evangelist the Rev. Jerry Falwell founded the conservative Christian campaigning organisation, the Moral Majority.[1] While its main purpose was domestic – to combat liberalism and permissiveness within America itself – the Moral Majority was also passionately Zionist, supporting the Israeli right wing's claim to a Greater Israel within its biblical boundaries. The roots of this conviction, central to the Moral Majority and to its successor organisations, lie in a particular interpretation of the Bible. In the Old Testament there are references to the Chosen People being returned to the Holy Land and the coming of the Messiah, but in the New Testament it is the Book of Revelation that forms the basis of Christian Zionist belief. This contains the prophecy that the Millennium and the Second Coming will happen when the Jews are not merely restored to the Holy Land but converted to Christianity and accept Christ as their Messiah. In other words, the Jews, not known for their enthusiasm for conversion, have literally to see the light, to accept a Second Coming to make up for their rejection of the first one.

From 1977, an alliance between the American religious right and the Israeli nationalist right began to form and it has endured to the present day.[2] On the face of it, it may seem bizarre that Israeli Jews should accept the friendship of those whose greatest hope is their conversion to Christianity. Yet the link has proved too important to both sides for them to let even this obstacle stand in its way. For the American religious right, a Jewish state in the biblical Holy Land, even if it has not yet become Christian, is a major step along the path set out in the Book of Revelation. For the Israeli right, the support of a grouping with such influence and voting power across the USA is far too useful to be sacrificed for a point of theology. The unspoken compromise appears to be that as long as the US Evangelicals leave the conversion of the Jews to God rather than man, the Israeli right is prepared to overlook its allies' ultimate goal. There could be no better proof of this unlikely pact than the words of Binyamin Netanyahu to a Washington Evangelical prayer breakfast in 1985:

I suggest that for those who know the history of Christian involvement in Zionism, there is nothing either surprising or new about the steadfast support given to Israel by believing Christians all over the world. For what after all is Zionism but the fulfilment of ancient prophecies? . . . And this dream, smouldering through two millennia, first burst forth in the Christian Zionism of the nineteenth century – a movement that paralleled and reinforced modern Jewish Zionism . . . Thus it was the impact of Christian Zionism on Western statesmen that helped modern Jewish Zionism achieve the rebirth of Israel.[3]

In the Moral Majority and its evangelical successor, the Christian Coalition, the Israeli right has had very powerful friends. The Protestant Evangelical churches form the largest religious grouping in America, and many of them hold firmly Christian Zionist beliefs. This helps explain the remarkable level of support these views enjoy among the American population as a whole. According to a poll carried out in 2006 by the respected Pew Forum on Religion and Public Life, 42 per cent of Americans believe that Israel was given by God to the Jewish people, and fully 35 per cent that Israel is part of the fulfilment of biblical prophecy about the Second Coming of Christ. These figures help explain the solidly pro-Israeli stance of US public opinion: the same Pew Forum survey found that 52 per cent of Americans sympathise more with Israel than with the Palestinians, while only 11 per cent thought the contrary. It has been calculated that biblical prophecy leads 33 million Americans to support Israel, a fact which explains why Israeli politicians are so eager to cultivate them. (Overall the Protestant faiths account for 51.3 per cent of the population, the Catholics for 23.9 per cent, and the Jews 1.7 per cent. These figures put the supposed wealth and power of the 'Jewish lobby' into some perspective.)[4]

Yet Christian Zionism is not an indigenous American plant. In this book we hope to examine how the movement flowered first in Britain in the

Evangelical Revival of the late eighteenth and early nineteenth centuries and was exported to America as it was fading at home. Yet it did survive sufficiently in Britain to influence a certain section of the ruling class who, whether for religious or political reasons, always played with the idea of a Jewish state on the shores of the Eastern Mediterranean.

Extraordinarily, the genesis of this movement can be traced to a single fascinating and unlikely figure, the Reverend Lewis Way (1772–1840), whose influence still reverberates today and whose story is the subject of this book. Educated at Eton and Oxford, Way was socially a polished and witty man. Paradoxically, he also believed passionately in Armageddon and the Apocalypse. However, his aim was not only to convert the Jews to speed the Second Coming, but, in preparation for this, to alleviate their oppressed condition throughout Europe.

Lewis Way did not realise his dream in his lifetime. Yet he left an important, if highly ambivalent, legacy. On the one hand, his determination to remind Christians of the debt they owed the Jews, which had been repaid only by persecution, touched a chord in the highest levels of government. In England, it helped create a philo-Semitic current, quickened by religious guilt, that led to the Balfour Declaration. On the other hand, his fundamentalist theology, carried to America after his death, became the direct inspiration for the apocalyptic Zionism of the Moral Majority. Which facet of Way's legacy – the moderate, humane one, or the fanatical, sectarian one – will ultimately prevail remains an unanswered question.

Lewis Way's work and travels shed a fascinating light on the contemporary Church, the condition of the Jews in Europe, and the politics of his time and our own. He devoted his great energies, his considerable fortune and ultimately his health to Christian Zionism. What grew from his work was to take over a century to reach fruition. 'Mighty oaks from small acorns grow' is an apt adage for Way's story in which trees were to play such an important and poignant part.

– One –

T hough he did not know it at the time, the extraordinary journey of Lewis Way began in early October 1799, when he was twenty-seven years old and working as a barrister in chambers in the Inner Temple. On that particular October day, a man called John Way happened to walk through the courtyard with his solicitor, Mr Edge, when his attention was struck by the name 'Lewis Way' painted on one of the doors. As he was not aware of any such relative, he sent the solicitor off to make inquiries about his namesake. Edge duly reported back that the young barrister was known as a man of probity and ability, and came of a well-connected, if not wealthy, family from Denham in Buckinghamshire. Later that month, John Way paid a call on Lewis Way in his chambers. The two men discovered they were not, even remotely, related, but, despite their age difference, they got on extremely well and found they had more than their surname in common.

John Way was sixty-seven years old. Now retired, he had been a confidential clerk and agent to the Lord Chief Justice, Lord Mansfield, and worked for him at Kenwood, the mansion he had built for himself on Hampstead Heath. By shrewd investment, no doubt advised by his employer, Way had acquired a considerable fortune. He was married but had no children and was very concerned about who or what cause should inherit his substantial legacy. In fact the reason for his being with his solicitor in the Inner Temple that day was to change his will to exclude a beneficiary whose behaviour he now considered unsuitable. Later it must have seemed to him as though the hand of God had brought the two Ways together. John Way was a deeply religious man and the hand of God was very important to him.[1]

Soon Lewis Way was regularly visiting John Way and his wife in their country house in Acton, a village he had frequently passed on his way home to Denham. Both men were devout Christians, John a Methodist and Lewis an Anglican with Evangelical sympathies. They were avid Bible-readers and found much to discuss and agree on. Originally Lewis Way had wanted to go into the Church but his father had been strongly against it. Though his maternal grandfather was the Rector of Denham and the living was in his gift, it had been decided that this should go to Lewis's not-so-bright younger brother. His father decreed that Lewis was 'too clever' for the Church and would find a more profitable living at the Bar. So, after his ten years at Eton, Lewis went up to Merton College, Oxford, in 1789 to read law. As an undergraduate his firm Evangelical beliefs did not inhibit him from enjoying himself socially, nor did his continuing biblical studies prevent him from writing and publishing comic verse. By all accounts he was, and remained, a charming and popular person. When he_graduated he was made a Fellow of the College and duly called to the Bar.[2]

Lewis Way had never enjoyed studying the law or practising it. Eventually it might provide a profitable living, but for a young barrister with very limited private means life was hard. Lewis's discontent was further fuelled by the fact that in 1798 on a visit to the Drewes, family friends in Devon, he had met and fallen in love with Mary Drewe. She was eighteen at the time and he was twenty-five. The Drewes were wealthy landed gentry and Lewis felt he could not propose marriage to their daughter in his present very limited circumstances.

Lewis's predicament with his professional and private life came to John Way's attention early in their relationship. Initially only aware of the professional problem, John Way suggested that he would subsidise Lewis to stand as Member of Parliament for Bridport in Dorset. John Way had been born and brought up there and had once had the ambition to stand there himself. Lewis, though grateful, had to tell his potential sponsor that he did not want a career in politics. John Way's next solution for his young protégé was marriage to a wealthy heiress. The one he had in mind was only a stone's throw away, the daughter of a wealthy and titled neighbour.

Again Lewis had to decline gratefully, and admitted he was in love with Mary Drewe, but unable to propose till his prospects were much improved. This problem was resolved by John Way writing him a cheque for £1,000 (approx £75,000 at today's value). The marriage took place on 31 December 1801 at Totnes in Devon.

The couple bought and lived in a small house in Westminster. Their first child, a son, was born in 1803 (subsequently three of their nine children were to die before the age of two). Lewis continued to try and make his way at the Bar. In a letter to his favourite aunt, he wrote:

. . . my friend Pell is really the only young lawyer I have heard of who could marry on his profession at 35, and he, poor fellow, has always been crossed in the attempt . . . He has made a fortune and wants a wife, I have got a wife and a fortune to make. I am learning economy and expect in time to become a miser.[3]

Before he died John Way had mentioned that he would like his fortune to be used 'to the glory of God' without stipulating exactly how 'God's glory' might best be served. His health was declining and he died on 18 August 1804, aged seventy-two. In his will, having made very adequate provision and income for his wife, a codicil bequeathed the residue of the estate to Lewis Way. This residue turned out to be a sum of £300,000 (approximately £23 million at today's value). Virtually overnight Lewis Way became a multi-millionaire. It came as a total surprise to him. The press were intrigued by the story and various inaccurate sums were mentioned about the size of the inheritance, as well as much facetiousness about the names of the deceased and his beneficiary, the *Leeds Mercury* commenting, 'Where there's a Will there's a Way'.[4] The discontented barrister suddenly became a millionaire celebrity. For the next six years Lewis Way was a man with a large fortune looking for a suitable cause to spend it on. In more normal times he and his growing family might have spent a small fraction of their wealth on a European tour, as had been the fashion. Britain, however, had been at war with France since 1793 and for the next twenty-two years – apart from a brief peace in 1802 – it was not safe for anybody British to travel on the mainland of Europe.

Meanwhile, in 1805, Lewis Way bought Stansted Park, a magnificent stately home in West Sussex, set in more than a thousand acres of parkland and forest with landscaping by Capability Brown. Way bought it to serve as a family home befitting his new status and with a shrewd eye to the future. It was both a good investment for some of John Way's fortune as well as a potential means of fulfilling his pious wishes. John Way had often talked of starting some form of religious college or foundation and Stansted would be ideal for this purpose. It was big enough and had its own chapel.

Without any regret Way abandoned the Inns of Court and spent the next six years restoring and refurbishing Stansted Park and leading the life of a country gentleman. His strong religious beliefs and numerous philanthropic donations brought him into contact with many of the leaders of the growing Evangelical movement: the Abolitionist William Wilberforce, the bankers Sir Thomas Baring and Henry Drummond, and the revivalist preachers Charles Simeon and Edward Irving. Way's greatest inspiration, however, was to come through the strange serendipity to which he seemed prone. In the winter of 1811, he was in Devon, visiting his in-laws, the Drewes, near Exmouth. Out riding nearby with a local friend, he came across an extraordinary building called *à la Ronde*. (It is still there, now owned by the National Trust.) It is a sixteen-sided building, designed and built in 1797 by Jane and Mary Parminter, two spinster cousins, to remind them of the Basilica of San Vitale in Ravenna which they had once visited. The interior of the building is even more extraordinary than its exterior. The rooms all surround a central octagonal hall, sixty feet high, its walls intricately decorated with shells and birds' feathers. There are no doors, only panels that slide back to lead to the rooms.

From his friend, Way learned that Mary Parminter still lived there, but that Jane, her older cousin and guardian, had recently died. Her will and the

6

lives of the two women were much gossiped about locally. Mary had been orphaned when a child and was fifteen years younger than Jane, but both were of very independent mind and considerable means. At a time when it was unheard of for women to travel on their own, Jane and Mary Parminter travelled throughout Europe together. After ten years of living abroad, only the turmoil on the Continent forced them to return to England in 1795. They were both devout Anglicans and after building *à la Ronde* they built a chapel nearby looking out over Exmouth Bay. They called it 'Point in View' and inside the chapel is the inscription 'Some point in view – we all pursue.'

Beside the chapel the Misses Parminter built almshouses and a small school, and endowed a fund whereby four 'worthy maiden ladies over 50' could live in the almshouses and one of them act as schoolmistress to six poor female children. The most unusual clause in the fund's deeds specified that if a candidate for the almshouses was a Jewess who had converted to Christianity she should receive preference. Likewise the children of Jewish parents would have preference over all others in selection for the school. The Misses Parminter certainly believed in the Millennium and the Second Coming. That this belief included the return of the Jews to the Holy Land was made clear and visible in the final sight pointed out to Lewis Way at *à la Ronde* – a fine line of oak trees beyond the chapel. It was a well-known local fact that Jane Parminter had added a recent codicil to her will that decreed, 'These oaks shall remain standing, and the hand of man shall not be raised against them till Israel returns and is restored to the Land of Promise.' This strange injunction became known well beyond that small corner of Devon; pamphlets were published about it, sermons preached and even verses written:

> List to the voice of the aged Trees
> Pass them not heedless by;
> I hear in the sound of the moaning breeze
> The earnest and heartfelt cry
> Of her who willed that these trees should stand
> Till the Jews should return to their Fatherland.[5]

Seeing the line of oaks and hearing about the codicil concerning them had an inspirational effect on Way. He already had a total belief in the Second Coming and was very familiar with the mystic conditions attached to it in the Book of Revelation. He suddenly realised that 'for God's glory' there could be no greater use of John Way's fortune than to use it for the conversion and restoration of the Jews and thus bring closer the Second Coming. Lewis Way had found his cause – his point in view.

– Two –

Lewis Way's revelation on the road to Exeter was, like so much else in his life, a strange mix of the spiritual and the fortuitous. It was not, however, untypical of its time. Britain in 1811 was in the throes of a major religious renewal, in part a response to two revolutions, the French and the industrial. In particular, the French Revolution had led to eighteen years of almost continuous warfare between Britain and France in which Britain had twice come very close to invasion. As so often happens in moments of great crisis, the response in many quarters was a rallying to religion. It was no coincidence that the Napoleonic Wars marked one of the high points of the British Evangelical revival.

By the early nineteenth century, the Evangelical movement, which had originated in John Wesley's preaching and the rise of Methodism, had been gathering pace for several decades. Being less concerned with doctrine than practice, Evangelicalism is hard to define. One key characteristic was a profound reverence for the literal text of the Bible, rather than complex interpretations. Another was a renewed emphasis on spreading the word of the Gospel. It was thus logical that the wave of new missionary societies founded at the turn of the nineteenth century – the London Missionary Society, the Church Missionary Society, the London Society for Promoting Christianity among the Jews – should become bastions of Evangelicalism. The movement also strongly emphasised the importance of an emotional closeness to Christ realised in a specific, revelatory conversion experience. All the great British Evangelicals – John Wesley, Charles Simeon, William Wilberforce – underwent a conversion experience, and Lewis Way's discovery of his 'Point in View' in Devon was clearly another such moment.[1]

British Evangelicalism was not limited to the Church of England, but embraced several other Protestant denominations, especially Wesley's movement, Methodism. All Evangelicals shared the same aim: to revive faith among populations alienated by the lax practice and neglect of parish duties of the eighteenth-century established Church. Increasingly, the poverty and social problems of the new industrial cities offered a further field for action. By the mid-nineteenth century, the Evangelicals' efforts had met with significant success. Methodism in particular tripled its numbers between 1801 and 1851, but church attendance in Evangelical Anglican parishes also rose appreciably. The moral earnestness, self-discipline and religious faith that were such features of Victorian Britain were largely the creation of the Evangelical movement.[2]

By the time Lewis Way embarked on his own particular mission, the most prominent Evangelical grouping was a predominantly lay one, the Clapham Sect. This was a network of able, well-connected and deeply pious men and women based in Clapham, then a pretty village just outside London. Wilberforce became the most famous of them, but important roles were also played by Zachary Macaulay, ex-governor of Sierra Leone and father of Thomas Babington Macaulay, Charles Grant, chairman of the East India Company, the banker Henry Thornton, the writer Hannah More, and the Cambridge clergyman Charles Simeon. Its greatest achievement was masterminding the great public campaign that led to the abolition of the slave trade in 1807, but it also threw its weight behind several other causes, such as prison reform, church building – and the restoration and conversion of the Jews.[3]

Another important aspect of Evangelicalism, but which pre-dated it and whose relations with it were often troubled, was millenarianism. This was the aspect with which Lewis Way would become most closely associated. As its name suggests, millenarianism is the belief in the advent of the Millennium and the Second Coming of Christ. It can be traced in Jewish religious literature at least as far back as the Book of Daniel. Its classic exposition, however, comes in verses 20 and 21 of the Book of Revelation, the last book of the New Testament.

There has been some mystery about its authorship, but it is usually attributed to St John the Apostle, writing in exile on the Island of Patmos towards the end of the first century AD. For those Evangelicals who take it literally, Revelation has always exerted a powerful appeal, since it offers them the certainty that their strenuous efforts to spread the Gospel will shortly pave the way for the reign of Christ.[4]

With extraordinarily powerful imagery, Revelation prophesies the imminent return of the Son of God and his apocalyptic battle against the forces of evil, led by Satan and the false prophet he has set up to lead mankind astray. This ends in Satan's defeat by his enemies, and the inauguration of the thousand years of his rule, the Millennium. Although the names are not specifically used, the apocalyptic battle has often been identified with Armageddon and the false prophet with Antichrist. After the thousand years, however, Revelation foretells Satan's return and gathering of a new army, which is swiftly destroyed by divine intervention. Revelation's final chapters describe the Last Judgement and the descent of the New Jerusalem from heaven to earth.

For centuries in the Christian world, in times of great suffering and crisis, millenarian movements had sprung up that saw these hardships as precursors of the Last Days – the Flagellants during the Black Death and the sixteenth-century German Anabaptists are just two of the most famous examples.

Less well known, but crucial to the story of Lewis Way, is that the French Revolution and Napoleonic Wars also spawned a series of millenarian sects and prophecies in both Britain and Europe. This is hardly surprising given that the Revolution and the twenty-two years of warfare it triggered formed one of the major upheavals of world history. In France, the king was executed by his own people and Christianity itself was attacked. Soon afterwards, the Revolution's heir, Napoleon, extended the French empire over most of Europe, throwing down monarchs from their thrones and creating new satellite states in their place. All the while, a war was raging that killed close to four million people.

To contemporaries of the Revolution and Napoleon, it seemed as if all the familiar landmarks – religion, the social order, national boundaries – were being torn up. Inevitably, some saw in this turmoil the long-foretold Armageddon and the approaching Millennium. By the early 1800s, the influential German mystics Jung Stilling and Adam Müller were predicting the imminence of the Second Coming. If the Napoleonic Wars could be seen as the Apocalypse, it followed that Napoleon was the Antichrist, and many contemporaries made this identification.[5] The novelist and socialite turned prophetess Baroness von Krüdener did so in her itinerant preaching in Germany, Switzerland and even eastern France.

This millenarianism was not confined to just one

side of the Channel. Britain was far from immune to the wave of war and revolution sweeping the Continent; she joined the conflict just one year after it started, in 1793, and, apart from one brief period, was continuously at war with France until 1814. In 1797 she was in grave peril from a combination of French invasion, radical subversion, naval mutiny and Irish rebellion. From 1803 to 1805 the invasion threat was repeated when Napoleon massed 170,000 troops at Boulogne. In such alarming times, apocalyptic preachers found a ready audience. In 1792, a middle-aged domestic servant, Joanna Southcott, announced that she was the 'woman clothed with the sun' described in verse 12 of Revelation who would bring forth the new Messiah. She prophesied the imminence of the Second Coming and attracted thousands of followers. Twenty-two years later, aged sixty-four, she proclaimed she was actually about to give birth to the Messiah, but she died shortly afterwards and her claims did not survive a post-mortem.[6]

1792 was a good year for British prophets. In February, a retired naval lieutenant called Richard Brothers declared himself to be the Prince of the Hebrews and the nephew of the Almighty, and preached the Second Coming to large crowds in London. Charged with sedition, he was committed to a private asylum in Islington, but on his release he rejoined a small band of faithful followers who stayed with him until his death in 1824. Another prophetic voice was William Blake, a far more important figure than Joanna Southcott or Richard Brothers. Like them, however, he had a radically Protestant upbringing and a deeply mystical turn of mind. He was profoundly influenced by the French Revolution and its effects. His poems are crowded with imagery from the Book of Revelation, none more so than 'Jerusalem', though the Heavenly City it invokes is not literal, but a metaphor for the regeneration of England.[7]

Millenarianism had another vital aspect, and it was this that spoke most clearly to Lewis Way. The Book of Revelation was commonly interpreted as predicting the conversion of the Jews to Christianity and their restoration to the Holy Land as a crucial element in the Second Coming. This view had deep roots in Britain, particularly associated with the seventeenth-century Puritans. Andrew Marvell, Cromwell's unofficial poet laureate, wrote, wisely after the Restoration, his famous 'To His Coy Mistress':

> Had we but world enough, and time,
> This coyness, lady, were no crime . . .
>   I would
> Love you ten years before the Flood,
> And you should, if you please, refuse
> Till the conversion of the Jews.

The allusion in that last line would have been perfectly understood by any literate English reader at the time, who would know his Bible and understand that the Chosen People were destined to return to the Holy Land and accept the Christian Messiah at his Second Coming. It would not of course happen overnight and Marvell's lover, impatient to win his lady, was not prepared to wait till the fulfilment of the prophecy.

It is significant that Lewis Way came from Puritan stock, with a great-grandfather, Benjamin Way, who had been removed as vicar of his parish and harshly persecuted for his radical religious views. To judge from accounts of his sermons his theology was both fundamentalist and apocalyptic, as his great-grandson's was to be a century later.[8]

Once again the millenarian upsurge during the French wars was accompanied by revived expectations for the conversion and restoration of the Jews. In Britain alone, between 1796 and 1800 no fewer than fifty books were published speculating on the Jews' return to the Holy Land. One event in particular helped stimulate this. In July 1798 Napoleon invaded Egypt to extend French power in the East. Having established himself there, the following February he turned north into Palestine. From Jerusalem, on 20 April 1799, he issued a proclamation to the Jews, 'the rightful heirs of Palestine', calling on their support and promising them in exchange a return to their homeland under French protection. Although this grandiloquent scheme came to nothing and Napoleon was soon forced to withdraw from the Middle East, to those who believed in such things it seemed a further sign of the approaching Millennium.[9]

It was against this background that the London Society for Promoting Christianity among the Jews was formed in 1809. From the beginning, the Society was a particularly prominent and fashionable organisation. Its first president was Lord Barham, a famous admiral and former Comptroller-General of the Navy. It was a clear sign of the links between the new Society, the Evangelicals and the Clapham Sect that William Wilberforce, a close friend of Barham through the campaign against the slave trade, was one of its vice-presidents. The Society's greatest social coup came in 1813, when the Duke of Kent, the third son of George III, agreed to become its patron. On 7 April that year, the Duke laid the foundation stone of the Society's missionary college, church and school at Palestine Place, Hackney, in the presence of a gathering of almost 20,000 people, including Barham, Wilberforce, the Lord Mayor of London, and Lords Bessborough, Crawford, Lindsay, Dundas and Erskine.[10]

The question does arise as to how many of this distinguished company had actually met or known a Jew, let alone one who wished to convert to Christianity. The Jews had been re-admitted into Britain in 1655, under the aegis of Cromwell, but

17

of the 20,000 who were there by 1813 the majority were of the lower orders, small shopkeepers, tailors and pedlars. There were a small number of wealthier merchants and financiers, mostly of Sephardic origin, who were well established in London.[11] There was some interest in these more exotic members of the Jewish community and a degree of assimilation was beginning to take place. In 1809, the year the Society was founded, there is an interesting account of a visit, organised by one of George III's sons, the Duke of Cambridge, when he went with his two brothers, the Dukes of Cumberland and Sussex, to the Great Synagogue in Duke's Place to see a Jewish service.

The synagogue was brilliantly illuminated and magnificently decorated for the occasion, and it was remarked that the royal brethren seemed most impressed by the beautiful singing of the choruses and the beautiful Jewesses in the gallery. They stayed the night in Finsbury Square with Mr. Abraham Goldsmid, who gave a banquet, followed by a concert, in their honour.[12]

Yet behind the impressive patronage and ambitions of the London Society lay the seeds of several future problems. One particular tension was evident within the Society from the beginning. This was between straightforward Evangelicals who did not believe in the imminence of the Second Coming and simply wished to preach Christianity to the

Jews, and millenarians who believed it was imminent and supported conversion and restoration in order to hasten it. The Society's Annual Report in 1810 firmly backed the first group: 'If nothing peculiar appeared in the aspect of the times – if neither Jews nor Christians believed the future restoration of Israel . . . still your Committee would urge the importance and propriety of establishing a Jewish Mission.'[13] These cautious words, however, didn't impress the Society's millenarian wing. As the Rev. Legh Richmond proclaimed in a sermon in November 1812:

We *know* indeed that the latter times approach, that the Jews *must* and *will* be restored; these things greatly animate us in exertion, and enliven our hearts in labour . . .[14]

In all this missionary fervour and talk of an imminent Second Coming, there was the delicate matter of the First Coming that had to be dealt with or ignored. The roots of Christian anti-Semitism, as opposed to Christian Zionism, lay in the accusation that it was the Jews, not the Romans, who were really responsible for the crucifixion of Christ. The London Society for the Promulgation of Christianity among the Jews skirted discreetly round this inflammatory subject.

A more immediate danger for the London Society was that, like most religious and missionary organisations then and now, it attracted its fair share of charlatans. The most notable was, embarrassingly, one of its founders, a converted German Jew called Joseph Frey. Arriving in Britain from Berlin in 1801, Frey soon set himself up as a missionary to the Jews, and was indeed the driving force behind the setting-up of the London Society in 1809. He was clearly an energetic preacher and fundraiser; in 1812 alone he delivered 279 sermons, which brought in £4,000. Unfortunately, his energies also extended to the less reputable fields of embezzlement and philandering, culminating in his discovery 'in a house of ill-repute in Ipswich'. The resulting scandal brought the Society into some disrepute, and it was mocked in pamphlets and in the press, though Frey was not actually ejected from it until 1816. To add to its woes, the previous year the Duke of Kent had resigned as its patron. The Duke gave his reason as unease at the Society's vigorous proselytising – somewhat inappropriately, he had sternly warned it against this in his speech inaugurating Palestine Place.[15]

By the time Lewis Way entered the scene, the London Society's early hopes had thus been seriously compromised. Its chief missionary had been exposed as a rogue, and despite the substantial sums raised since its foundation, by 1815 it was £14,000 in debt. For all its efforts, of the approximately 20,000 Jews then in the UK, it had managed to convert just 100 between 1809 and 1814.[16] From a glittering start, misfortune and mismanagement had brought it close to collapse.

Lewis Way's first contact with the London Society had sprung directly from his realisation of his mission. On returning from Devon in 1811, he had immediately asked an old friend, Thomas Burgess, Bishop of St David's, if there was any missionary organisation devoted to the Jews, and Burgess had directed him to the Society. Way quickly realised that before he could begin his real work, the Society had first to be rescued, and he threw himself into this task with ferocious energy. He was swiftly added to the list of vice-presidents, and by 1814 was working with Wilberforce, his fellow-Claphamite Charles Simeon, and Lord Barham to set the Society on a firmer footing. Up until then it had been a joint enterprise between Anglicans and Nonconformists, but to avoid interdenominational squabbling Way and his colleagues turned it into a purely Church of England organisation. This also solved the problem of finding a replacement for the Duke of Kent as Patron; Way provided not one but two Bishops, Bishop Burgess of St David's and Henry Ryder, Bishop of Gloucester.

Way's greatest early service to the London Society, however, was financial. In 1815 he proposed the banker and MP Sir Thomas Baring as its President, but on finding it was in debt by £14,000 Baring refused. On the spot Way put a draft for £10,000 into Baring's hand, thus conquering his objections, and making it much easier to pay off the remaining £4,000. Lewis Way saw this as the means of using John Way's bequest as it was intended 'to the glory of God'. Certainly it saved the Society from an early demise.[17]

By 1816, the London Society was reorganised and solvent. Palestine Place, covering five acres off the Cambridge Road on the edge of the East End, was rapidly being developed. The Jews' Chapel had been completed by 1814 and around it was built a boys' and a girls' school, administrative buildings and housing for the use of missionaries. The Society continued to promulgate Christianity among the Jews, even though the number of the converted averaged only around seven a year. Many Jews, however, made use of the educational facilities on offer without committing themselves to a final conversion.

Missionary Societies also need colleges to train their missionaries, and here too Way had a contribution to make. With typical generosity, he offered his own home at Stansted Park for the purpose, as a Hebrew College. To enjoy legal status it would need a charter, but this was a slow and cumbersome process. In the meantime Way opened his house to any Jews who wished to convert to Christianity as preparation for future missionary work. In the course of the next year, a remarkable and exotic group of converts and would-be evangelists gathered at Stansted.

The most prominent was the Rev. Nehemiah Solomon, originally a Rabbi from Berlin who had converted to Christianity there. His wife, however, had refused to follow suit and begun divorce proceedings, so he had abandoned her and his children and made his way to Britain. Arriving at Stansted, he was taught Latin and Greek, and swiftly ordained as a Deacon by the Bishop of Gloucester. An even odder case was the Sultan Kattegarry, a Tartar Muslim nobleman from the Crimea who had studied at Edinburgh and converted there to the Kirk of Scotland, later travelling south and switching to the Church of England.[18]

Other house-guests had shorter stays. Soon after arrival at Stansted, sixteen young converted Jews heard a false rumour that Lewis Way had gone bankrupt, whereupon they left hurriedly, taking with them all the valuables they could lay their hands on, in particular the household's silver spoons. Rather disloyally, since his father Zachary was a friend of Way, the young Macaulay penned some caustic lines on the incident:

Each, says the Proverb, has his taste. 'Tis true
Marsh loves a controversy, Coates a play,
Bennet a felon, Lewis Way a Jew,
The Jew, the silver spoons of Lewis Way.[19]

To sceptics, and religious opponents, Lewis Way and his band of enthusiasts would always provide good ammunition. Despite this, it is remarkable how much benevolent interest they aroused, and how many powerful connections they made and retained. At this time George Canning, the future prime minister, was a frequent guest, as well as Way's uncle, Edward Cooke, the secretary of the foreign minister Lord Castlereagh. The household was even visited by the Duke of Clarence, the future King William IV.[20]

This Anglo-Jewish-Christian idyll was not destined to last long. The great events of the outside world would soon make themselves felt even in West Sussex. Napoleon had finally been defeated at Waterloo, and for the first time in twenty-two years Lewis Way could extend his field of action to the Continent, and link up with like-minded Evangelicals across the Channel. Above all, even in the traditionally cynical world of power politics it seemed that Christian principles were finally to triumph -- in September 1815, Czar Alexander I of Russia created the Holy Alliance. For Lewis Way, the most like-minded Evangelical across the Channel was now the Czar of Russia, and Way decided that part of his personal mission must be to meet him.

– Three –

At the time Lewis Way was having these thoughts at Stansted, Alexander I of Russia was at the pinnacle of his controversial and stormy reign. Born in 1777, Alexander had had a troubled childhood and youth, dominated by the mutual loathing between his father, the Czarevich Paul, and his grandmother, the Empress Catherine the Great. After Catherine's death, the unstable Paul lasted only five years on the Russian throne before being murdered in a palace coup and replaced by Alexander. Although it is highly unlikely that Alexander approved his father's assassination, he had certainly encouraged his deposition. A feeling of responsibility for Paul's death left him with a permanent sense of guilt and sinfulness, which no doubt influenced his later turning to mystical religion.[1]

The first phase of Alexander's reign was marked by high hopes and grand plans for enlightened reform. For his subjects, the tall, fair and charming Alexander was a considerable improvement on the diminutive, pug-faced and paranoid Paul. Initial schemes to introduce a constitution and abolish serfdom proved unsuccessful, but major steps were taken to creating a state education system. The

Jewish Statute of 1804 also attempted to improve the lot of Russia's Jews.[2]

The decisive factor that shaped Alexander's reign, however, was the struggle against Napoleon. In 1805, Russian troops marched into Central Europe to confront the French, and were heavily defeated. By 1807, Alexander had little option but to make peace, and entered an uneasy alliance with France. Over the next few years, however, this progressively broke down, and in June 1812 Napoleon invaded Russia with a vast army of 600,000 men. He occupied Moscow, but the Russians obstinately refused to come to terms, even burning much of the city to make it untenable for the French as a base of operations. In October, Napoleon withdrew; already depleted by the march to Moscow, his forces were wrecked by a combination of Russian harassment, the collapse of their supply system, and an unseasonably early winter. Fewer than 100,000 survived. The retreat from Moscow not only saved Russia, it turned the tide against Napoleon for good.

Much of this was Alexander's own achievement. Often hesitant and indecisive in the past, he displayed great courage and tenacity in the face of the French invasion. His obstinate refusal to make peace as long as any French forces remained on Russian soil inspired his own people and eventually placed the invaders in an impossible situation. Far from becoming one more victim of Napoleon, Alexander had become his conqueror, and the prestige he acquired from this never left him.

The root of Alexander's transformation in 1812, however, was neither political nor military, but religious. At the most critical moment of the crisis, he had a conversion experience. There are several versions of how this happened, but the most common is that he asked his close friend Prince Alexander Golitsyn how he could stay calm at such a time, to which Golitsyn replied that this was because he trusted in God and the Scriptures. At this moment Golitsyn's Bible dropped to the floor and fell open at the extremely apposite Psalm 91: 'He will cover you with his feathers, and under his wings you will find refuge; his faithfulness will be your shield and rampart.' Shortly after this, before Alexander left to join his troops at the front, a woman, reported to be Countess Tolstoy, gained admission to his study, gave him her blessing, and thrust a folded paper into his hand. Thinking it a petition, Alexander put it into his pocket without reading it. Later, when he looked at it, he saw it was the 91st Psalm. Alexander saw in this coincidence the hand of God, and from that moment became a born-again Christian.[3]

From this standpoint it was easy for the Czar to interpret the French invasion in religious terms, as a titanic struggle between Christ and his elect, and the forces of evil and darkness. He had already had Napoleon denounced as Antichrist in 1806, and had not revoked this even after making peace with him at Tilsit.[4] With Napoleon as Antichrist, the Napoleonic Wars stood revealed as the Apocalypse, and the Millennium could not be far off. Alexander's revelation came from the 91st Psalm and the burning of Moscow, Lewis Way's from the oak trees of an eccentric English spinster, but both arrived at an identical religious destination.

Over the next three years this religion came to dominate not only the Czar's personal life but also his public actions. It inspired him in the military campaigns that pushed Napoleon back into France and eventually forced his abdication in April 1814. Above all, it shaped his ideas on the subsequent peace. Instinctively, he felt that this should be based on Christian principles, as the only true basis for the happiness of Europe and her peoples. For some months, however, he refrained from publicising these views.

In the summer of 1815 he changed his mind. The catalyst for this was the Baroness Julie von Krüdener, a mystic and prophetess, who for the past eight years had proclaimed all over Central Europe that Napoleon was Antichrist and that the Millennium was at hand. Like Joanna Southcott, she believed she was the 'woman clothed in the sun' of Revelation; unlike Joanna Southcott, she was aristocratic and cosmopolitan and, before her own conversion experience in 1807, a novelist and socialite. On 4

June 1815, she secured a meeting with Alexander at Heilbronn, and exhorted him for three hours never to falter, as the Elect of God, in his task of destroying Christ's enemies – an apposite point as Napoleon had just escaped from Elba. Profoundly moved, Alexander wept copiously. Now, for a short but highly significant period, Mme von Krudener became his spiritual directress.[5]

The main fruit of Alexander's collaboration with Mme von Krüdener was the Holy Alliance. In September 1815, as the Congress of Vienna, called to decide the post-war settlement, was drawing to a close, the Czar presented a remarkable document to his two principal allies, Emperor Francis I of Austria and King Frederick William III of Prussia. It was a draft treaty by which the three rulers would dedicate themselves to 'settling the rules to be observed by the Powers, in their reciprocal relations, upon the sublime truths which the Holy Religion of Our Saviour teaches'. Essentially, it was a blueprint for transforming Europe into a Christian commonwealth, whose rulers would henceforth base their relations with each other and with their subjects on the precepts of the Gospels. With some misgivings, but feeling Alexander was too powerful to refuse, Francis and Frederick William signed the pact on 26 September.

The Holy Alliance, as it was soon dubbed, had a decidedly mixed reaction from contemporaries. It has generally been regarded either, as Castlereagh put it, as 'a piece of sublime mysticism and nonsense' or as a hypocritical ploy intended by Alexander to mask his real goal of Russian territorial expansion. Yet neither viewpoint can explain away the considerable evidence that the Czar's sentiments, though visionary, were both sincere and consistent. His correspondence with his closest confidants, particularly Golitsyn, makes this plain.[6]

Remarkably, Alexander may have wished to consolidate the Holy Alliance by reunifying all the Christian denominations into a single Church. As he himself once said to a Lutheran pastor: 'Personally, it makes no difference to me what confession people belong to, since every church is equally valid.'[7] This ecumenical goal is reflected in the text of the Holy Alliance itself. It exhorted the signatories to 'consider themselves all as members of one and the same Christian nation . . . thus confessing that the Christian world, of which they and their people form a part, has in reality no other Sovereign than Him to whom alone power really belongs.' Reconciling Catholicism, Protestantism and Orthodoxy was a highly visionary aim, but Alexander may well have believed that in forming the Holy Alliance he was laying the first stone of a pan-Christian European commonwealth.

For this commonwealth to flourish, all its members would need a sound knowledge of the basic tenets of Christianity, which for Alexander could only be based on individual Bible reading. This became the purpose of another extraordinary initiative. In Russia, access to the Bible had been limited to the Orthodox clergy. In 1812, however, Alexander gave his backing to one of the major new British missionary organisations, the British and Foreign Bible Society, in a campaign to distribute a Russian translation of the New Testament to as many of his subjects as possible. Within ten years, the Society had sold 464,000 copies of its Russian Bible, distributed a further 800,000 for free, and translated it into forty different languages and dialects of the Russian Empire.[8]

Many Russians, not least the Orthodox Church whose monopoly was being challenged in this way, must have found the Czar's religious views bizarre, even revolutionary. To one group of Christians, however, his literalist interpretation of the Gospels, his ardent desire to spread them, and his conviction of an imminent Millennium, would have been thoroughly familiar. In all the essential aspects of faith, Alexander was a Protestant Evangelical in Russian Orthodox clothing, and one Protestant Evangelical in particular took note of the fact.

From Stansted, Lewis Way had been watching Alexander's progress with mounting fascination. The two men's paths had almost crossed in 1814, when Alexander had visited England in the wake of Napoleon's abdication and been received as a hero.

In between the festivities, the Czar had made a point of meeting Way's fellow-Evangelical, the anti-slavery campaigner Thomas Clarkson, a deputation from the British and Foreign Bible Society, and several Quakers. Already, through their shared religious preoccupations, Alexander's circle and Way's were beginning to overlap.

The proclamation of the Holy Alliance was an important sign to Way that the moment had now arrived to start in earnest, at an international level, the conversion and restoration of the Jews. He was convinced that Alexander was the perfect ally he needed to undertake it. There was only one problem. The Czar's mystical and millenarian outlook was well known, but whether the Jews themselves played any part in it still remained mysterious. In early 1817, however, he dropped a hint that they did. On Easter Sunday, he issued an ukase, or decree, removing all the civil disabilities normally imposed on Russian Jews from those who converted to Christianity. These converts, to be formed into a Society of Christian Israelites, were also promised free land grants in the Crimea, which had recently been conquered by Russia and which the government was keen to colonise. This was clearly not restoration – the Crimea was hardly the Holy Land – but the Czar was obviously keen to evangelise the Jews, or, as one contemporary more poetically put it, 'to bring these wandering sheep into the fold of Christ'.[9]

For Lewis Way, Alexander's ukase was a call to action. Now that the London Society, thanks to his own generosity, was back on a firm footing, it was eager to send out a representative to the Continent to report both on the condition of the Jews and on the prospects for setting up missions to them. W. T. Gidney, a later secretary and historian of the Society, wrote about these overseas ambitions:

The Jews abroad are not surrounded by the same pure and sound Christian principles and life as those in England, and their spiritual need is proportionately greater.[10]

Even for missionaries it seems 'the grass is always greener . . .', but the remark could be seen as an ingenious and patriotic excuse for the poor results that the Society had had with conversions at home. For Way, however, this was an ideal opportunity well suited to his inquiring mind and Evangelical zeal. It would also provide a cover for him to travel on into Russia. There, he would gain an interview with Alexander, and enlist his help in his own plans for the Jews.

The London Society was delighted by Way's proposal of himself for its mission – not least because he was willing to travel at his own expense. It was agreed that he would travel to Holland, Germany and Russia. His plan to meet the Czar he kept carefully to himself. He made one exception to this that gives insight into the resources that he could draw on to smooth his path. To obtain an official introduction to the Czar, Way invoked the good offices of his uncle, the Rt. Hon. Edward Cooke, Lord Castlereagh's secretary at the Foreign Office, who had met Alexander on his visit to London in 1814.

The fact that Cooke was ideally placed to further his nephew's project did not, however, mean that he was automatically willing to do so. In fact, Cooke took a highly critical view of Lewis Way's plans. An acrimonious correspondence followed in which he accused his nephew of virtually disinheriting his family to waste his fortune on the Jews:

I have been unwilling to believe that you can possibly be guilty of so unnatural a Measure, but, at the same time, I am aware of your Visionary Flightiness . . . It appears to me that, for a long time since, you have bid adieu to the beggarly Elements of Common Sense and Discretion! But I have still flattered myself that you would one day come back to them, and reconcile yourself to the best Gifts of Providence.

Way took grave exception to his uncle's reference to 'Visionary Flightiness', claiming that this placed his own religion 'upon a footing with Joanna Southcott', and a family rupture seemed imminent. Yet in the end Way's charm and persuasive powers prevailed and the letter of introduction to Alexander was forthcoming.[11]

In planning and setting out on a journey in the

early nineteenth century time could not be of the essence, and Way went to great lengths to ensure the success of his mission. For some time he had felt he would gain more respect if he had himself ordained. With his knowledge of theology and the Bible and his close friendship with the bishops of Gloucester and St David's, his ordination had presented little problem, and he had become a deacon in 1816 and a priest the following year. Next, he had commissioned the translation and publication of the New Testament into Hebrew for use on his travels, and, at a more practical level, he had designed a specially sprung coach with two very high, outward sloping wheels for travelling on rough or marshy land. Way hoped that this coach would afford him and his companions some small degree of comfort and space on their journey. By October 1817, he was finally ready to embark.

Journeying the length of Central and Eastern Europe – the last stages in the depths of a Russian winter – was a major undertaking, but nothing seems to have daunted Way. He had never travelled on the Continent before and was leaving behind his home and his family, a son, three daughters and a pregnant wife, with his date of return unknown. Realising how much he would miss them, he commissioned John Downman, a fashionable portrait painter, to do a portrait of Mary, and a separate one of his four children. Both are now in the British Museum. Way carried them everywhere with him in a large red wallet. Just before he set off, he commissioned from James Leakey a portrait of himself with the wallet under his arm.

If Lewis Way is seen as a Don Quixote figure, he certainly took an extraordinary mixture of Sancho Panzas with him on his journey. The Rev. Nehemiah Solomon, whom the London Society had chosen to open and maintain a mission with the Crimean community of converts, was one. Another was Sultan Kattegarry, who would act as interpreter in Russia. With a more straightforward background, acting as Way's secretary, was Charles Maberley, who drew well and would record some of the journey. Finally, there was the Reverend Robert Cox, representing the London Society, who spoke no French, had considerable trouble communicating and returned home earlier than the others.

Before they sailed from Harwich to Holland, friends and families of the travellers and representatives of the London Society were summoned to nearby Colchester for several farewell services and dinners. One of those who attended was Way's cousin and namesake, the Rev. Lewis Way of Spencer Grange, who recorded the occasion in his diary. After the service he writes of seeing Sultan Kattegarry embrace the Rev. Nehemiah Solomon and 'with tears in his eyes, say in broken English 'Go my brother and preach the blessed gospel of our Lord

Jesus Christ to your brethren who are in darkness.'
It struck me as very remarkable,' he continued, 'to
see a convert from the religion of Mahomet give
such an exhortation to a converted rabbi ordained a
Deacon by a Bishop of the Church of England.'[12]

– Four –

On 8 August 1817, Lewis Way, his strangely assorted company and their coach sailed for Holland. It was their intention to visit the major Jewish communities all across Northern Europe on the way to St Petersburg. This was no small task; of a total European Jewish population of roughly 1.75 million in 1800, 40,000 lived on the travellers' path in Holland, then 420,000 in Central Europe, and finally over a million in the parts of Poland recently annexed by Russia. This tiny proportion of the overall European population of 187 million was still a substantial number of souls to study and evangelise.[1]

Above all, Way's journey took place at a critical moment for European Jewry. The Revolutionary and Napoleonic Wars had dismantled swathes of the centuries-old restrictions and burdens placed upon the Jews throughout the Continent. Wherever French armies had gained control, especially in Italy and the German states, the Enlightenment principles of religious toleration and equality of opportunity were proclaimed. In these areas Jews had generally been admitted to full civic rights on the same basis as their Christian neighbours. The most tangible signs of their separate and inferior status, the ghetto walls, had often actually been knocked down by the French sappers, with bands playing as if at a festival or review.[2]

With the fall of Napoleon, this emancipation was immediately threatened. By no means were all the monarchs and statesmen who gathered for the Congress of Vienna in late 1814 reactionary or anti-Semitic. Prussia had voluntarily abolished most of the restrictions on her Jews in 1812, and at Vienna her leading ministers, Hardenberg and Humboldt, attempted to get Jewish emancipation included in the constitution of the new German Confederation that replaced the Napoleonic dispensation. They were foiled, however, by an underhand trick. The delegates who wished to revert to the *status quo ante* altered the article guaranteeing the Jews 'all rights heretofore accorded them in the several states' to 'all rights heretofore accorded them by the several states'. Since in most cases the German states had been forced to grant Jewish emancipation after the French invasion, they could argue that this had not been granted by themselves but by the French, thus making it non-binding. Although not all the states of the Confederation took advantage of this loophole, a number did – in Frankfurt efforts were made to confine Jews once more to the ghetto, and in Bavaria and Saxony residence restrictions on them were re-imposed.[3]

Arriving on the Continent to encounter this

revival of old prejudices, Lewis Way's reaction was forthright. He was horrified by the persecutions meted out by Christians to Jews over the centuries, and convinced that they should be treated as fellow human beings with equal rights. Only once Jews had learned to trust Christians, he argued, could genuine conversion be attempted, through friendly argument and without constraint. 'What I plead for on behalf of this distressed people', he wrote, 'is civil and political freedom – an entrance into the great family of Society. It is vain to ask the Jews to become Christians otherwise!' The agitation to revoke the Jews' civil status that he witnessed on his European journey he repudiated with disdain, drawing a typically Evangelical parallel between Jewish emancipation and Wilberforce's anti-slavery campaign:

If in some countries fanatical or self-interested clamours against the emancipation of the Jews can still be heard, they are no more representative of public opinion than the infuriated declamations of some colonial plantation-owners against the suppression of black slavery and the slave trade.[4]

As Way soon found out, the condition of the Jews varied considerably in the countries through which he travelled widely. At each stage of his journey he wrote a report on this to the London Society, which printed them in its journal, *The Jewish Expositor*, as they arrived. In Holland, the emancipation brought by the French had broadly been maintained after

1815. In Hanover and Prussia, where the party next stopped, the condition of the Jewish communities had also not reverted to their oppressive pre-Napoleonic state, though Jews were still barred from entrance to the universities and most professions. One of the problems Way encountered was that some of the upper-class Jews had indeed converted, but purely for civil and economic advantage. To convert Jews for genuinely religious reasons would, he admitted: 'be a labour of love which requires the faith of Abraham, the fervour of Paul and the patience of Job himself'.[5]

Way's activities at each stage of his journey were a curious mixture of fact-finding forays, conversations on religion with well-disposed Jews and Christians, socialising with local high society, and carefully judged proselytising. In Rotterdam a leader of the Jewish community said to him: 'Sir, the only way to make converts of our nation is to show them personal kindness, and prove that you consider them entitled to the common respect paid to people of all other religions' – Way's own sentiments exactly. En route to Berlin, on 19 September, Way and his company stayed in Deventer, a small Dutch border town, and joined the Jewish community there for a meal to celebrate the end of Yom Kippur, the Day of Atonement.[6]

Once settled in the Prussian capital, Way distributed the Gospels in Hebrew to any Jews willing to receive them, and held open house every morning for any of them, especially students from the university, who showed interest in his mission. He also observed the first steps of Reform Judaism. Probably sensing in it a rival, he dismissed it scornfully as a 'substitute for a synagogue'.[7] Way also made sure to cultivate the great and the powerful, and the means he employed again illustrate the reach of his connections. The British Ambassador to Prussia was George Rose, a near neighbour in Sussex and firm Evangelical, and Way was soon introduced by him at court. He made a life-long friend of the twenty-two-year-old Crown Prince, Frederick William, who, like the Czar, was a firm believer in the divine right of kings and involved in Christian mysticism. Way wrote to his wife about being entertained by the king's cousin:

I had not a moment to write to you from Posen where we were hospitably received by the Princess Louise of Posen-Radziwill, who has palaces at Berlin, Posen and Warsaw. I had the honour of always sitting next to her at dinner, and a more delightful lady I have not seen.[8]

The party was detained in Berlin longer than planned by the Reverend Nehemiah Solomon's Berlin past catching up with him. This arrived in the form of his Jewish father-in-law, angrily flourishing the divorce settlement that now seemed not to have been agreed to or signed. If the terms were not improved his wife would return to him. Solomon's shrewd response was to declare that if his wife returned she would straightaway have to accompany him to Russia. Clearly the terms of the divorce were preferable to an instant trip to Russia, and the Rev. Solomon was free to continue his journey unaccompanied. Way wrote to Mary, 'It was well the Solomon affair was settled before we left for Russia for his father-in-law would certainly have followed us to the ends of the earth!'[9]

The route to St Petersburg lay along the Baltic coast, in what had been Poland before the Partition of 1795 made it part of Russia. It was at this stage that Charles Maberley, the secretary, made the only surviving sketch of the extraordinary coach, unfortunately only from the back. Somewhere on the coast near Memel, Way reported a remarkable experience:

I was left in the middle of a sandy wilderness . . .The carriage had stopped and the horses were taken off . . . A caravan of Jewish merchants, whom we had previously passed along the road, overtook us, and stopped at the same place: five of them came round the carriage, when they saw me hold out a book which was an Old Testament in Hebrew; from this they each read part of the fifty-third of Isaiah. I then took out my New Testaments and turned to the third of John, which they read in as audible a manner as a roaring wind and sea would allow. They were evidently struck with the occurrence, each took a copy and received them with apparent thankfulness.

What refreshments I had, I divided among them, and they all bowed very respectfully as they drank out of the same glass. We had no common language, but the word of God can speak for itself.[10]

On 2 December they reached Riga, still with another 350 miles to go to St Petersburg. Five days later Way wrote to his mother: 'The winter being now set in, wheels are no longer useful, so we left the carriage and the Jew with the Rev. Cox at Riga, and Sultan, Maberley and I have passed two delightful days in a sledge travelling faster than an English Mail . . . We hope to reach our destination in two days.'[11] In fact it took four days, the outside temperature was minus 20 degrees, and they lived mainly on soup and rusks. Yet despite all the vicissitudes, judging by his letters Way always kept his good humour – even when he finally arrived in St Petersburg

Back view of Rev^d L Way's Carriage in The Baltic – when passing The Curische Nehrung

Lewis Way's specially designed carriage on the road to Riga, 1817. Drawn by his secretary, Charles Maberley.

to find the Czar was in Moscow, a further 400 miles away. While they waited for the rest of the party to join them Way read the mail that awaited him from his wife and family. Mary was well and due to have the baby in six weeks.

Just before Christmas they arrived in Moscow, its burning in 1812 still very visible. Way described the city as 'half-rebuilt, half ruins'. A house had been engaged for them. It was called Toutolmin House, a long, low building, built entirely of fir trunks. Maberley made a drawing of it, with an inscription revealing his shaky command of Russian: 'This house was situated in the district of Moscow called Metrereou-lochpreecheestinker.'[12] It was from there Way wrote a Christmas letter to Mary. It shows once again his extraordinary knack for getting to know the right people to further his cause: the British Ambassador, Prince Golitsyn, now minister for religious affairs

Way's party stayed in Moscow at Toutoulmin House,
one of the wooden buildings hastily thrown up after the fire
of 1812. Drawn by Charles Maberley.

and public instruction; and V. M. Popov, Golitsyn's chief departmental head:

My Dearest Mary,

Some of my letters must have prepared you to receive one dated from hence and you will be happy to know that, as the journey was indispensable, it is performed . . . I dined the first two days with our ambassador, Lord Cathcart, who took very kindly to me and gave me a general invitation to his house and table. He had prepared the way with all parties here, and nothing can be more gracious or satisfactory than the reception I have met with from Popoff and Prince Galitzin . . . I am sure they will always be my friends, and I am sure I will possess their confidence and be enabled to do good with them.

I begin now to think more and more of you and our little friend who is coming. If there are two boys, one is to be Alexander and the other Basil, for those are the names of my good friends Popoff and Galitzin . . . If it should prove a female, she can be Catherine or Louisa, whichever you shall prefer.

I shall willingly stay in this interesting and delightful country to see the Jews out of their troubles, and then I shall come home, or you must come out in the summer, but my plans cannot be fixed for six weeks to come – so be patient! Xmas day with us is Epiphany with the Russians, so that on the same day that Christ was announced to the Gentiles we have done all in our power to announce him to the Jews. My letter to the Emperor is dated on that day.

Ever your old Wandering Jew,
Lewis.[13]

The letter Lewis Way wrote that Christmas Day, asking for a meeting with the Czar, was probably the most crucial one of his life. If Alexander agreed to see him, his mission would at least get to the next stage; if he did not, all his hopes would be dashed and a journey of 1,500 miles have been made in vain. The next few days were spent on a knife edge. The first response from the Kremlin was a refusal. Undaunted, Way returned to the palace and left his card and the letter from his uncle Edward Cooke. The next day, Thursday, 3/15 January, a reply arrived:

His Imperial Majesty the Czar desires to see the Revd Mr Way *to-day at half-past six* after noon. Therefore His Excellency the Prince Golitsyn will send the bearer of this at six of the clock precisely to the Revd Mr Lewis Way in order that he can accompany him to the palace of the Czar and to show him the precise room where it will be necessary to wait upon His Majesty's order for the audience.[14]

– Five –

I n fact, it was somewhat after six o'clock when Prince Golitsyn's courier arrived. Lewis Way followed him to the New Palace in the Kremlin and then through a maze of corridors crowded with guards and pages to an attic room where he waited for ten minutes. He then went down more corridors and was ushered through a large door and found himself

in a large room in the presence of the first Potentate on the face of the globe. To my own utter surprise (nervous as I sometimes feel) I was perfectly calm and collected, and had I been ever so much embarrassed, the gracious manner of His Majesty would have set me at my ease. He was standing at the fireplace by a large screen, dressed in upper military coat without star, and in high boots. I bowed as soon as he observed me, when he at once came forward and met me not far from the door. He immediately took me by the hand in the most easy and condescending manner and said in English 'Mr. Way, I am very happy to make your acquaintance. I have heard much of you from our friends and I wish we may be known to each other.'[1]

These last words no doubt referred to Golitsyn and Popov, and maybe also to British Evangelicals like Thomas Clarkson, who Alexander had met on his stay in London in 1814. They reinforce the impression of a strong fundamentalist Christian network of which both Way and the Czar were a part. Yet good references alone could not have made the meeting a success without the immediate empathy that sprang up between the two men. Despite their very different stations in life, Alexander and Way were both intelligent, personable, exceptionally charming men, and obsessed with biblical prophecy. In every sense, it was a match made in heaven.

Czar Alexander I, 'the first Potentate on the face of the globe'. Painted by George Dawe.

Way now proceeded, as briefly as possible, to explain his mission. As he later wrote to Mary, 'His Majesty being deaf, made me sit quite close to him, which gave me a full opportunity of observing the traits of his benevolent and animated countenance.' At the age of forty, tall, handsome and with a military bearing, the Czar must have seemed to his visitor every inch an emperor. Yet Way, 'calm and collected', four years older than the Czar, was not intimidated, and clearly made an excellent impression. As a result the Czar granted Way three more long interviews during his stay in Moscow, which cemented a genuine friendship.[2]

When he travelled to Russia, Way could not have realised just how exactly Alexander's views on the future dovetailed with his own. Central to this was the Czar's conviction, steadily growing since 1812, that he was living on the threshold of the Last Days. As Thomas Clarkson observed at a subsequent meeting with Alexander in 1818: 'He himself was clearly of the opinion that the Peaceable Times prophesied of in the Holy Scriptures were hastening on, and that they would most assuredly come to pass.'[3] Since the Millennium was so closely linked to the conversion and restoration of the Jews, Way did all he could to strengthen his new friend's conviction. After a long discussion of Revelation with the Czar, he argued forcefully, contrary to more conventional Christians, that it predicted an imminent and terrestrial Second

Coming: 'Your Majesty observes that "a new earth" cannot be supposed to be in Heaven, and the City is represented as "coming down" instead of going up – therefore it seems to relate to a glorious state here below.'[4]

The key question about these meetings is whether Way discussed with the Czar the actual restoration of the Jews to the Holy Land. In his version of what transpired he implied that he did not: 'The Emperor conversed with me most fully and freely upon Jews, Gentiles, personal experiences, etc.,' he wrote. 'Not once in all my conversations with him did he ever refer to politics . . . what most delighted me was the full conviction of the spirituality of his mind.'[5]

For once, it seems, Way was being disingenuous. It would appear that the restoration of the Jews was discussed, but through the medium of biblical prophecy rather than contemporary power politics. For a prudent politician like the Czar, this presented an important advantage. It meant that he could express his support in principle for restoration and his conviction that it was imminent, without immediately committing himself to a policy that would be, to say the least, controversial. However, Way left a significant hint that the more practical aspects of restoration may have been raised. Towards the end of his written account of his meetings with Alexander there is an additional marginal note in Latin – *memoranda et tacenda* (things to be remembered and kept secret).[6] Perhaps politics were discussed, but Way was diplomatic enough not to commit what was said to paper.

A further entry reveals the atmosphere of Way's interviews with the Czar, and the extent to which Alexander was taken by the notion of becoming the protector and restorer of the Jews. The two men were reading together Isaiah 44, in which God says of King Cyrus of Persia, who allowed the Jews back to the Holy Land after the Babylonian Captivity: 'He is my shepherd, and shall perform all my pleasure: even saying to Jerusalem, Thou shalt be built; and to the Temple, Thy foundation shall be laid.' At that moment Alexander and Way looked at each other, and realised each had had the same thought, that Alexander was destined to be the modern Cyrus.[7]

This incident must have become known to Alexander's confidants, for in an undated letter clearly written at the time, Mme von Krudener's daughter Juliette, also a prophetess and close to the Czar, urged him even more explicitly to emulate the Persian king:

Sire, you are not only a Cyrus who must protect the return of the people of God to Jerusalem; your call extends even further. A second David, you must show mankind the meaning of a monarchy living in God and united with the priesthood; in a word what it is to be a leader of peoples who can say with St Paul: 'It is no longer I who live, but Christ lives in me!'[8]

The language and the aims may seem far-fetched, but they become less so in the light of another of Alexander's projects at this time, sponsoring a different religious migration into his own empire. In the summer of 1817 he charged Golitsyn with organising the journey of thousands of Christian millenarians from Alsace, German Switzerland, Baden and Württemberg who wished to settle under his rule. By the end of that July, 10,300 had arrived in Russia. Some were clearly keen to travel further. A few years later, in April 1820, the sceptical French Ambassador referred in a despatch to: 'mystical Lutherans who are now all the rage here and have come from Swabia to found colonies in Russia and then been sent towards the Caucasus, saying they are delighted by this since it brings them closer to Jerusalem, soon to be the centre of Christianity after the conversion of the Jews.' With one group of his subjects, the 'Christian Israelites', Alexander had been pursuing a similar policy since March 1817; indeed, it was the news of this that had set Lewis Way on his path to Russia. One community had already been given land in the Crimea, and it was to minister to them that the Rev. Nehemiah Solomon had been instructed by the London Society to travel.[9]

Part of the Czar's motivation in the case of both the Christian millenarians and Israelites was the need to colonise and consolidate vast areas of southern Russia recently conquered from the Turks.

Yet orchestrating a migration within Russia, even towards its extreme limits, was one thing, extending it beyond her frontiers, which restoring the Jews would involve, was quite another. At best it would involve an extremely difficult negotiation, and at worst war, with the Ottoman empire, of which Palestine formed a part. The second option was something Alexander was absolutely unprepared to contemplate. The demise of the Turks and the partition of their empire had been widely predicted for half a century, and one of Russia's main strategic aims was to gain control of Constantinople and thus access to the Mediterranean for her fleets, but the Czar's Ottoman policy from 1812 until his death was resolutely peaceful.[10] In part this was because he knew that Russia was exhausted by the struggle against Napoleon and incapable of sustaining a further conflict with the Turks, but his decade's experience of war and his religious conversion had made him a genuine pacifist. Having finally overthrown the Antichrist Napoleon, he believed he was introducing an era of universal peace.

This is borne out by the Czar's actions after the publication of the text of the Holy Alliance. The Turks were immediately concerned that it was aimed against Islam and presaged an attack on their dominions. Certainly Mme von Krüdener viewed it that way and consistently urged Alexander to undertake a crusade to liberate the Holy Places. The Czar would have no truck with such notions, and in March 1816 sent a circular to all the European courts to be communicated to the Ottomans, to calm their fears:

The unique and exclusive aim of the alliance can only be the maintenance of peace and the strengthening of all the moral interests of the peoples whom it has pleased Divine Providence to unite under the banner of the Cross. An act of this nature could not possibly of itself imply any hostile intentions towards peoples who do not have the good fortune to be Christians . . . Still less could an act of this character imply any project of conquest, since its goal can never be achieved by force of arms.[11]

Alexander clearly managed to find a way to reconcile his religious aspiration for the restoration of the Jews with his reluctance, at least in the short term, to antagonise the Ottoman empire. The answer to this paradox lay in the belief he shared with Lewis Way that the Millennium was imminent. Since the conversion and restoration of the Jews was near at hand, all the Czar had to do was to await the workings of Divine Providence. This perfectly illustrates Alexander's refined blend of mysticism and realism. It was very convenient to have a religious reason to counter those, like Mme von Krudener, who urged potentially dangerous political actions. If the international situation changed and the restoration of the Jews became a useful weapon to use against the Turks, one suspects the Czar would have revised his timetable for the Millennium to suit the circumstances.

On several occasions Alexander was candid about his thinking to his religious confidants. In July 1814 he had met the German mystic Jung Stilling, who told him that he would 'surely be the instrument by which a refuge in the East would be opened to Christians'. Alexander's reply was that 'he could predict nothing in advance and that at present he would not even move his little finger', but that 'he would obey with all his soul the moment the Lord gave the sign'.[12] His most forthright statement on the subject, however, was made to Lewis Way at the end of their first meeting:

My wishes for the return of the Jews are as warm as your own . . . but . . . there are many clashing interests. But you may be assured that I will do all in my power to assist it. I consider your coming to Russia as a providential concurrence of circumstances – each must do his part, and in time, with the blessing of God, all will be achieved.[13]

In the end there was little to choose between Way's approach and the Czar's. Way also believed that the conversion and restoration of the Jews would be God's work, and that the most any human could do was to nudge the process along. Later, however, Way was to link biblical prophecy specifically to the demise of the Ottoman empire. In a controversial pamphlet in 1822, he explicitly argued that the imminent collapse of the Turkish empire was foretold in Revelation:

. . . if the exhaustion of the Turkish power be signified by the drying up of the Euphratean waters under the sixth vial of the Apocalypse, all of which appears not only plausible, but in the highest degree probable; then, indeed, though we know neither the *day*, nor the *hour*, the *time* is come, when . . . those disciples who are not in darkness . . . [ought] to be even now, 'like unto men that wait for their Lord'.[14]

Finally, Alexander and Way did agree on one very practical step to further their aspirations. One of the regular gatherings of the great powers that had been provided for by the Congress of Vienna was due to take place the following autumn at Aix-la-Chapelle. Alexander was determined to place the situation of the Jews before this Congress. But restoration and its basis in biblical prophecy would have to be downplayed, as it was unlikely to appeal to hard-headed politicians like Metternich and Castlereagh. Instead the humanitarian aspect of Way's mission should be urged – the continuing emancipation of the Jews and the eradication of Christian prejudices against them. In the atmosphere of anti-Semitic backlash in many European states where recently granted Jewish rights were being contested, that was a sufficiently difficult project.

Alexander had reached the conclusion that the best person to plead the cause of the Jews at Aix-la-Chapelle would be Lewis Way himself. At their final meeting the two men worked out a plan together.

Way's intention had been to leave Moscow and proceed to the Crimea, see the Reverend Solomon installed in the mission there, then to return home as quickly as possible. Alexander was also going to the Crimea in the spring to visit one of the colonies of 'Christian Israelites'. He arranged to meet Way there. After the Crimea they would meet again at Aix in the autumn and together draw up a memorandum setting out their project.

For Way, even as the Czar's representative, addressing the crowned heads of Europe and their ministers was a daunting prospect, but difficult to refuse. Pleading for the rights of a wronged people and for their return to an ancient homeland would be the apogee of his mission. He would not just be doing Alexander's work but God's. He decided he would go to the Crimea and to Aix but in the interval between the two he would return to Stansted. He had already been away for four months and the new baby was due imminently.

At this stage of Way's journey its missionary aspect became most evident. Between Moscow and the Crimea he and his party stopped at numerous towns with Jewish communities and Way addressed large gatherings, with Sultan Kattegarry acting as interpreter. In Minsk they found a large Jewish community which seemed reluctant to listen to Way's message. When he made a courtesy call on the police chief, he mentioned this. The official summoned

a company of dragoons who, in Way's report to the
London Society,

escorted 200 of the choicest Israelites to the synagogue to listen to me. There were increasing sounds of irritation when-
ever the words 'sin' and 'saviour' were mentioned. Hitherto
we had tried nothing but bush-fighting and skirmishes, but
here we are in the midst of the enemy, and verily had a brisk
encounter . . .[15]

For Way, this meeting was the culmination of his career as an actual missionary, and it strengthened his
conviction that he stood on the threshold of great
events. He expressed this in his description of the
Rev. Solomon, who followed him in preaching a sermon to the Minsk elders:

A Christian deacon addressing an assembly of 200 of the des-
cendants of Abraham, is a phenomenon which the church has
not witnessed, perhaps, since the apostolic age, and which all
the efforts of a rich and peaceful society has not been able to
produce in nine years of uninterrupted labour for the welfare
of the Jews in England. So true is it, that prophets have no
honour in their own land, and so excellent and so binding is
the *last commandment*, 'Go ye into all the world'.[16]

It was not till he reached Odessa, after a 950-
mile journey, that Way learned in a letter from Mary
that there had been an addition to the family. The
Christian names of his friends Popov and Golitsyn,
however, had not been memorialised in Hampshire,

as Mary had produced another daughter, christened Louisa Catherine after the Princess of Prussia. She was already two months old. The reply he wrote to his wife contained a sentence that best epitomises the core of Way's equable and benign disposition: 'I find happiness at all times everywhere by expecting it at all times nowhere.'[17]

Way now pressed on to the Crimea, saw the Rev. Solomon installed in his mission and met members of the 'Christian Israelite' community. He also met Karaite Jews, adherents of a fundamentalist creed dating back to the ninth century. They believed in a purely literal interpretation of the Old Testament and ignored the subsequent man-made accretions of the Talmud and the Mishnah. They also accepted both Jesus and Mohammed as prophets. For them it was perhaps no great leap to actual conversion, as this also ensured their community a government subsidy as well as the personal interest of the Czar himself.

Alexander arrived in the Crimea in May 1818 and Way had an audience with him on the 18th at Government House in Simferopol. He reports Alexander as being as warm and friendly as before and greeting him with 'Sit down and tell me where you have been and what you have seen.' Sitting close again because of Alexander's deafness, Way outlined his journey and they discussed their 'Jewish and Christian concerns'. Way noted Alexander's particular interest in the Karaite Jews: 'He had been that very morning in the Synagogue and conversed with many Jews in their houses.'[18] There is no record of the reaction of these Crimean Jews to the Czar of all the Russias turning up unannounced on their doorsteps for a theological discussion.

When Way told him that he was intent on returning home before going on to Aix-la-Chapelle, the Czar pressed him fervently to remain in the Crimea. The Karaites had need of him. They needed further Christian instruction: 'You have been given a germ here, and you must stay and inoculate it.' Way wrote apologetically to his wife, 'It is impossible to describe the animation and affability of his Majesty's manner . . .' Way ended his letter resignedly, 'As a Quaker says, "having followed the sheep, I must now follow the tail."'[19] Presumably Mary was familiar with this saying. So Way stayed in the Crimea and, with the Reverend Solomon, preached to their flock and its tail till it was time to set out for Aix-la-Chapelle.

Sultan Kattegarry, himself a Crimean Tartar, stayed on in his old homeland before returning separately to England. Now there was only Way and his secretary Charles Maberley in the coach. With time finally on their hands they decided to take the scenic route. As they travelled back through Galicia, Silesia and Moravia, Way wrote of being delighted to be back in the land of chairs, tables and comfortable beds. When they reached Prague, Way visited synagogues and the famous Jewish cemetery of which he left a remarkable description:

The Jews' burial ground is the most extraordinary place I have ever visited. In it are not to say *a great* many graves because nothing short of millions can convey any idea of what there must be collected in that spot of death and decay and earthly oblivion. Its gravestones sink by their own weight to their necks and assume every fantastic position. The stones have accumulated to such an extent that no ingenuity could add one in anywhere, even cornerways. Imagine this almost completely matted and hidden by a dense thicket of knotted, dwarf, gnarled elder trees which struggle up through, and often have raised stones in their arms – and you have a notion of the very strangest scene I know of.

I cannot describe the singular sensations and ideas that thronged my mind . . . There is something to me affecting in this place, the extraordinary story of this people as a nation – their suffering and persecutions and tortures in the darker ages, their dispersion as individuals and unity as a people were all suggested at this *locale*. And this crowding together as it were for refuge after death from a world which held them in abhorrence, struck me as peculiarly melancholy and touching.[20]

By mid-July Way had reached Vienna and a packet of 'over twenty letters, none of which contained bad news'. From there the travellers headed to Geneva, as he had promised to show Maberley Mont Blanc and Chamonix. This done, they went on to Paris arriving there in late September. Way had now been away for eleven months and wrote an apologetic letter to Mary for not returning or bringing her over, but he had so much work to prepare 'for what you justly term the Great Crisis. At least I shall have done my duty and used an occasion, which may never occur again.'[21]

From Paris Way travelled a roundabout, cross-country route to Aix-la-Chapelle (today's Aachen). He could not resist visiting the great cathedral cities of the Rhineland and went via Frankfurt, Coblenz and Cologne, reaching Aix in early November. For centuries Aix had been an independent Imperial city, but in 1807 it became part of the artificially created Kingdom of Westphalia under Napoleon's brother, Jerome. In 1815, after the Congress of Vienna, it was incorporated into the kingdom of Prussia. Still only a medium-sized provincial town, it could not rival Vienna as a location for an international congress. It was quickly filled, not just with the European monarchs and their chief ministers, but with a host of lobbyists like Clarkson the anti-slavery campaigner, mountebanks, entertainers and cranks of all political and religious persuasions. Lewis Way was definitely not included in the last category. His credentials were impeccable. He was not only a friend of the Czar, and there under his personal aegis, but also known to many of his compatriots at Aix. His ally George Rose, the ambassador to Berlin, and even the Duke of Kent, who was then living in Germany, greeted him warmly.

Despite the work still to do and his nervousness about its final presentation, Way realised it would be impolitic totally to ignore this glittering social life around him. He found time to write Mary:

I was at Duke William's (the Prussian Crown Prince) concert with all the monarchs, and last night at Lord Castlereagh's, with whom I dine in half-an-hour . . . A few nights since I was at the Duke of Wellington's Soirée, where I met all the Sovereigns. Dear Alexander shook me by the paw like an old friend! And I drank the health of Old Eton with former Eton-ians in Champagne.[22]

When Way mentions meeting 'all the sovereigns', he omitted to mention that his own was missing. George III still remained in Windsor Castle closely guarded by his doctors.

Most of Way's time was now spent with Alexan-der compiling the manifesto they would present to the Congress. It was divided into three sections that would be presented in three booklets. As Way sum-marised them, they were:

1. Concordance of Scripture testimony to the return of Jews.
2. State of public opinion on their civil emancipation etc.
3. Concessions and advantages to the Jew and Gentile result-ing thence.[23]

What is remarkable about the manifesto, given the prudence Alexander and Way had adopted as their rule, was not how little it referred to biblical prophecy and the restoration of the Jews, but how much. The document was intended, after all, not just for the Czar's two fellow crowned heads at Aix-la-Chapelle, Francis I of Austria and Frederick William III of Prussia, but for the leading statesmen of Europe – Metternich, Castlereagh, Wellington, Hardenberg and Richelieu. Although judiciously phrased, Way's preface clearly linked the recent Napoleonic Wars with the conflicts described in Revelation and the return of the Jews to their homeland:

I would not dare to claim . . . that the four dominant Powers to whom Europe owes the benefits of peace, are personally prefigured in the seventh chapter of the Apocalypse. But it is evident to all who read and believe in the Scriptures, that just such an interval of repose, succeeding to political and moral upheavals which have shaken every State down to its foundations, and made the civilized world tremble for its existence, precisely matches the period in which the tribes of Israel shall be sealed by the word of God, and in which, as Jesus Christ himself says, *their deliverance is at hand.*[24]

The main thrust of the manifesto, however, concerned how in the interim the legal and social position of the Jews could be improved. Here Way, the fundamentalist Christian, ironically recommended the precepts of the Enlightenment and the French Revolution. The Jews should henceforth be admitted to all civil and social rights, especially those of property, he argued, on exactly the same basis as their non-Jewish compatriots. In those states where this remained problematic – those parts of Germany Way himself had visited – their emancipation should be introduced more slowly, but according to a fixed schedule. In return for full citizenship, the Jews for their part would become subject to military service and any tax exemptions they had previously enjoyed would be abolished. Way also advocated the encouragement of agriculture for a people who had always been associated with the world of commerce. He reasoned that the Jews were originally an agricultural people and only their expulsion from the Holy Land and subsequent persecution and exclusion had forced them to develop a faculty for usury and trade.[25]

It was an extraordinary feat for Way to produce this manifesto in French and at high pressure in little more than two weeks. He wrote to Mary:

I have done my duty and shall rejoice to return to my own dear home and comforts . . . I came to serve God and he has crowned and blessed me. The Emperor is dearer than ever. He has had and approved all my papers and plans, and will do all in his power. The Lord bless him! I have been engaged all morning as his private secretary for Foreign Affairs.[26]

Now he had to wait anxiously till 21 November, the penultimate day of the Congress, to address the assembled monarchs and their ministers. Though highly nervous and speaking in French, in which he was not entirely fluent, Way's gifts as an inspiring preacher and orator stood him in good stead. His own extraordinary story – his wealth and closeness to the Czar – would have been known to most of his audience and added to his charisma. He pleaded the Jewish cause under the headings on which he had organised the booklets. He called for tolerance and Christian charity as preached, but not yet practised, by so-called Christian nations. At one point he broke into English:

What I plead for on behalf of this distressed people is civil and political freedom – an entrance into the great family of Society. It is vain to ask the Jews to become Christians otherwise!

Reverting to French, Way's central plea was for a general edict supporting Jewish emancipation:

. . . a general edict drawn up by the sovereign powers, setting out the civil and political rights that the Jews should receive as citizens, is much to be desired, to encourage them in their good feelings towards their Christian brothers, to impose a uniform character on measures that have been partially adopted, and to put the entire community on the footing to which each party has equally well-founded claims.

He could not resist a final biblical flourish:

An edict could go forth from this Assembly of Sovereigns, by which, to use the words of Holy Writ, 'a country shall be conceived in a day, and a nation shall be born in an instant.'[27]

Way's arguments, oratory and personality clearly moved the Assembly. He did not get his edict, but the representatives of the five great powers did sign a protocol cautiously endorsing his programme:

. . . without adopting entirely all the views of the author of this document, the conference has acknowledged the general tendency and the laudable aim of his proposals. The Austrian and Prussian signatories have declared themselves ready to provide all the clarifications on the state of the question in both monarchies necessary to resolve a problem of equal importance both to the statesman and to the friend of humanity.[28]

The protocol was signed by the chief ministers of each power – Metternich for Austria, Hardenberg and Bernstorff for Prussia, Capodistrias and Nesselrode for Russia, Richelieu for France, and Wellington and Castlereagh for Britain. Way, elated, wrote to Mary: 'It is certain that such an appeal has not been made for the poor Jews since the days of Mordecai and Esther.'[29]

In retrospect, Way's delight was premature. For all his eloquence, he had only managed to extract from the Congress a general, and entirely non-binding, statement of support rather than any concrete measures. In fact, the Congress of Vienna had issued a similar statement recommending the 'amelioration' of the condition of the Jews in the German states three years previously. However, the fact that at the first European Congress since Vienna the

Jewish cause had been argued so forcefully, showed that the pressure for emancipation was not about to dissipate. Above all, Lewis Way had firmly placed the situation of the Jews, and perhaps even a glimpse of their restoration, before the assembled monarchs and their ministers. He had achieved the goal he had set himself, 'of fixing the attention of the great monarchs upon a people who form the key to the history of the world'.[30]

Aix-la-Chapelle was to be the high point of Lewis Way's career. He had stated clearly his mission before the leading monarchs of Europe, with the backing of the most powerful one of them all, and the prospects for the future looked encouraging. After the Congress ended, he spent several days discussing the next stage of the project with the Czar. Remarkably, it appears from Way's account of their conversations that at this point Alexander not only explicitly gave his support to the restoration of the Jews to Palestine, but also to their civil emancipation, by stages, in Russia itself.[31] The two men then parted, Alexander to return to Russia, Way via Brussels to England. They never saw each other again.

Even now Way did not manage to return immediately to his family. As he wrote to Mary, he encountered a serious delay at Brussels:

due to the decrepitude of my carriage, which is fairly worn out in the service. One wheel has come off three times, two of the springs are broken, and not a timber sound. I shall change or mend it as fast as possible, and fly to you by night and day; but I am sure you would rather have me a day later with my legs and arms, than a day sooner without.[32]

After a thirteen-month absence, Way finally arrived at Stansted, physically intact. He was just in time for Christmas with the family and to meet his daughter, Louisa Catherine, for the first time.

– Six –

After his triumph at Aix-la-Chapelle, Lewis Way now had to turn his mind to the tasks ahead. If the restoration of the Jews was in God's hands – and the Czar's – the immediate labour to which he could turn his efforts was their conversion. Missionary activity now became the guiding theme of his work. Way threw himself into this with his usual boundless energy. Within two weeks of his return from the Continent he attended a meeting at William Wilberforce's house in Surrey to discuss the way forward. If missionary endeavours were to flourish, trained missionaries were needed. Way resurrected his previous plan to turn part of Stansted Park into a missionary college for Jews and Gentiles. His conscience, however, continued to trouble him about further depriving his family of their legacy. His friends reassured him and a memorandum of the meetings states:

The times imperiously called for such an institution . . . Mr. Way's fortune was not an hereditary one, but was unexpectedly given to him by God, and the person who left it wished to have it employed in promoting the glory of God . . . The Journey which Mr. Way has made and the result of it show that God is blessing him in his work. If he had *only* procured the Protocol it would have been an ample proof of this.[1]

Shortly after this Way drew up a petition to obtain a charter from the Crown for the foundation of such a college and submitted it to the prime minister, Lord Liverpool, a personal friend. He felt confident that with his own connection with the Royal Family through the Duke of Kent, his request would be speedily granted.

Way now devoted himself to putting the finishing touches to the decoration of the chapel at Stansted. Its consecration took place on 25 January 1819, and the service was taken by his two good friends, Bishop Ryder of Gloucester and Bishop Burgess of St David's. The chapel was crammed and an unexpected visitor was the poet John Keats. On holiday nearby with his friend and chronicler, Charles Brown, he saw a notice for the ceremony in a local newspaper. They would both have been aware of Way's celebrity, and Brown wrote in his diary, 'Tomorrow we shall go to Stansted to see Mr. Way's Chapel consecrated by the two Bigwigs of Gloucester and St David's.' Not surprisingly, the service was extremely long and, according to Brown, Keats was 'not amused'. His attention, however, was clearly captured by the unique stained-glass windows with their Jewish iconography and there is clear reference to this in both his subsequent poems, 'The Eve of St Agnes' and 'The Eve of St Mark'.[2]

While Way waited for a favourable answer from the government about the charter for his college, he decided to undertake a mission himself. In August

1819, under the auspices of the London Society, he went on a preaching tour in the West Country. He continued to Ireland, where, in Dublin, he made his most impressive convert, much to the dismay of Trinity College. Alexander McCaul had received his MA there at the age of eighteen and was considered their most brilliant graduate for many years in both theology and languages. McCaul heard Way preach a sermon in Dublin that 'entirely altered the whole course of his life'.[3] He went to Stansted, studied Hebrew and joined the London Society, and his obvious ability led to his being appointed, at the age of twenty-two, head of the Warsaw Mission.

McCaul's later work took him into Western Russia, and in the footsteps of Way, with letters of introduction, he also had meetings with Czar Alexander. The problem they discussed, a legacy of both the Czar's and Way's work, had become a crucial one to the prospects for converting the Jews. In Russia and Poland, as in England, the Jews who converted to Christianity frequently found themselves unacceptable both to their fellow-Jews and their new co-religionists. Many became isolated and unemployed, and their new faith was sorely tried. The solution that McCaul attempted, with the Czar's support, was to create workshops where the converts became skilled in new trades. The London Society, in its headquarters at Palestine Place, had already introduced the same process. McCaul, after ten years' work in

Eastern Europe that included translating the New Testament into Yiddish, returned to England and eventually became Prebendary of St Paul's Cathedral and Professor of Hebrew at London University.[4]

Although Way returned to Stansted from his tour with a talented new collaborator, the first ominous signs appeared that all was not well with his plans. The most important concerned the Czar. Although there was no breach, communications with Alexander slowly petered out. Contemporaries and subsequent historians have often accused the Czar of dilettantism, but it would be unfair to add the conversion and restoration of the Jews to the list of his discarded causes. He remained deeply interested in the subject to the end of life. After 1818, however, a series of disturbing international and domestic developments forced him to concentrate his energies elsewhere.

Aix-la-Chapelle had seen the Czar at the height of his power, the arbiter of a Europe that seemed ripe for implementing his humanitarian and visionary schemes. Within months this prospect had soured. The revolutionary and Napoleonic spirit, apparently defeated at Waterloo, began to show dangerous signs of life again. In March 1819, just three months after Aix-la-Chapelle, the pro-Russian publicist August von Kotzebue was assassinated in Mannheim by a radical German student. The following September, partial elections in France showed a major swing to the left, and in February 1820 the king's nephew, the duc de Berry, was murdered at the Paris Opera by a Bonapartist. The following month revolution broke out in Spain, and four months after that in Naples. Most alarming of all for Alexander, in November 1820 his favourite guards regiment, the Semenovsky, mutinied briefly in St Petersburg.[5]

Although radical propaganda played little part in the Semenovsky regiment's mutiny, Alexander's more conservative advisers, egged on by Metternich, did everything to convince him that it had. Combined with the other bad news coming in from all over Europe, this wrought a significant change in the Czar. The confident and benevolent liberal gave way to an embattled and disillusioned conservative. From 1819 until his death in December 1825, Alexander's domestic policy grew steadily more repressive and his taste for foreign adventures dissipated.

This was a major blow to Lewis Way and his mission. Although through his own efforts he had gained considerable attention for his cause, and could still boast powerful patrons from William Wilberforce to the Crown Prince of Prussia, his trump card had been the Czar. Alexander had brought him to Aix-la-Chapelle, and with Alexander lay the only hope of an eventual restoration of the Jews. Certainly missionary activities could be pursued, and missionary colleges founded, under the aegis of the London Society, but the heady perspectives that the

Czar's patronage had encouraged were now rapidly shrinking.

The following years were disappointing ones for Way. Having used all his influence to gain the charter for Stansted, there was not yet positive news. Though still a celebrity and much visited by his distinguished circle, Way had clearly lost some of his influence in high places. A backlash against the London Society had begun within the Anglican establishment. Despite Way's efforts, the disgrace of Joseph Frey had not been forgotten, and this was to figure prominently in a stinging attack on the Society published in 1825 by the influential clergyman Henry Handley Norris. The Duke of Kent had withdrawn his patronage; his reasons were not officially given, but he had clearly become concerned the Society was proselytising too aggressively.[6]

Way decided that if he could not use Stansted for his original purpose he would leave it – at least for the time being. He rented it out for two years as a means of augmenting his much reduced fortune. In times of stress travel acted as a tonic for him and he decided on a European grand tour. Despite straitened circumstances, he spared little expense, and the number of travellers and the amount of their baggage gives a remarkable insight into the style in which the wealthy journeyed on the Continent at the time. The family, Lewis, Mary and their six children, were divided up between a large coach and a phaeton. They took with them a tutor for Albert, now seventeen and an accomplished illustrator, a governess for their five daughters, ranging in age from Drusilla, eighteen, to the baby of two, as well as a coachman, a postillion, a butler and a cook, fourteen people in all, not to mention their luggage. Heavier items, like Mrs Way's piano, Drusilla's harp and two ponies for the children were sent by sea to Nice. On their overland journey through France, Albert drew and illustrated the stories of the younger girls, and a packet of these small story-books still

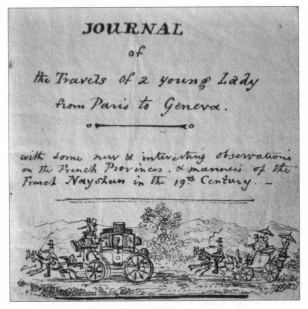

The Way family on their travels.
Drawing by Lewis Way's eldest son, Albert.

survives. In Nice they rented a villa and Way soon set about his missionary activities. Mary wrote to her mother:

Lewis has dined at Mr. Avidois, the rich Jew Banker, who, with the Chief Rabbi, has had two discussions with him, but with little apparent effect. The Rabbi is a most noble, venerable-looking man. We intend to visit the synagogue on Saturday. Nice abounds in Gentlemen, and not less than six English Clergymen.[7]

Way preached a sermon in the English church and began writing a tract entitled *Thoughts on the Scriptural Expectations of the Christian Church* for publication by the London Society. He wrote it under the pseudonym 'Basilicus', and it was to have a dramatic effect on the Society and his relations with it.

Way's philanthropic activities were not confined purely to the religious sphere. Upset by the poverty and unemployment he saw around him, he met with the local commune and gave them a substantial sum to help build a road along the seafront.[8] In his honour it was called the *Promenade des Anglais*. It is ironic that while little remains of Lewis Way's efforts to convert the Jews, a small act of charity to which he probably gave little thought has created one of the best-known landmarks of today's French Riviera.

Even in the south of France, Way remained in close touch with the London Society, and in this way his second great missionary journey was conceived.

The Society had asked him to investigate the condition of the Jewish communities along the French Mediterranean, as he had done on his last journey through Northern Europe, and he had already begun this in Nice. Now the Society wanted him to travel to the fringes of the Holy Land itself, to Syria, and look at the possibility of establishing a missionary college on the slopes of Mount Lebanon. Reassuringly, the Society knew Way could again be relied upon to pay his own expenses. He agreed to go for the opportunity this would provide to achieve his dearest wish and see Jerusalem. However, he refused to contemplate the lengthy separation from his family that the previous expedition had entailed. This time he would travel through Italy with his wife and children before taking ship at Naples, and Albert would come along with him on the voyage to the East.

The family set off in the early spring of 1823 and after visiting Florence split up. Mary and the four younger children set up house in Lucca, while the two oldest children, Drusilla and Albert, accompanied by Way's younger sister, Catherine, known as Aunt Kitty, moved on to Rome. From there Albert wrote to his mother:

It is a most handsome city, clean, streets all flagged, myriads of palaces with the appearance of prisons. We went to the Jews' quarter, though they are separated in this part of the town, they enjoy many more privileges than under the Tuscan government. The synagogue is a neat, pretty little building. The Rabbi was ill but his son and family received us courteously in the garret story of a most miserable and filthy abode, and accepted books.[9]

To show they were nothing if not ecumenical, the Ways' next religious engagement was an audience with the Pope, Pius VII, famous for having defied and been imprisoned by Napoleon. Way presented the Pope with a copy of his *Mémoires sur l'État des Israélites*. The Pope professed interest in both his book and his work and promised him introductions to influential people on Mount Lebanon. Drusilla was less impressed by the celebrated but diminutive Pope. She wrote to her mother:

We have lived here whole centuries in a day. I have been introduced to the Pope and the Neapolitan Ambassador. The Pope was dressed in the most dirty, snuffy old flannel dressing-gown imaginable. He was very courteous, but his appearance was abject. At a ball we attended we saw twenty Cardinals.[10]

Since his imprisonment the Pope had been in poor health and Way's was one of his last audiences before he died. Way did however draw his attention to a scene that had deeply shocked him. It was a tradition in Rome that every Sunday 300 Jews were forcibly compelled to listen to the preaching of a monk at a service at St Angelo Pescari. He wrote indignantly to Mary: 'This is an old law revived, as well as others, against this long-suffering people.'[11] Way obviously saw his own preaching in a different light – he had clearly forgotten the dragoons in Minsk.

Drusilla wanted to accompany her father to the Holy Land, but he had been advised that finding accommodation for a single woman would be too difficult. Instead she went to join her mother and sisters in Lucca, while her father and brother went on to Genoa. There, before sailing for Syria, they were joined by a Mr Lewis, an Irish member of the Society, who was an excellent linguist. Their intention was to land at Jaffa and then travel the 37 miles overland to Jerusalem. Unfortunately the boat was not allowed to dock there due to an outbreak of plague in the area. It continued north and they disembarked at Sidon, deciding to go straight to Mount Lebanon to search for a suitable location for the missionary college. They would have to see Jerusalem on the homeward journey.

Among several letters of introduction, Way had one to a figure who would dominate his stay in the East, the famous Lady Hester Stanhope. The brilliant and imperious niece of Pitt the Younger, Lady Hester had acted as her uncle's confidante and hostess at 10 Downing Street during his last years as prime minister. Pitt's death in 1806 had been the first of a series of bereavements that had determined her to leave England and travel to the East. First in the company of a younger lover, then alone, she had explored Palestine, Syria and the Lebanon, survived an attack of plague and become the first European woman to visit Palmyra. In 1814 she settled on Mount Lebanon, which remained her home for the rest of her life.[12]

Most important to Lewis Way was the fact that Lady Hester's religious beliefs almost exactly mirrored his own. Like his, they also dated back to the period of apocalyptic anxiety and expectation brought about by the French Revolution. In 1795, Lady Hester's curiosity had been aroused by the preaching of the prophet Richard Brothers, the former naval lieutenant, self-styled Prince of the Hebrews and nephew of the Almighty. She met him, and he predicted that she would travel to the East, spend seven years in the desert, and would then lead the Jews back to Jerusalem, paving the way for the Millennium. Perched in her fastness on Mount Lebanon, a figure of bafflement and awe to the local Lebanese, Lady Hester came to believe, like Joanna Southcott and Mme von Krüdener, that she was the 'woman clothed with the sun' of the Book of Revelation. In her stables, immaculately groomed, she kept two horses on which, she was convinced, she and the Messiah would soon ride into the Holy City.[13]

Lewis Way sent off his letter of introduction and immediately received back an invitation for himself, Albert and Mr Lewis to visit at her home on Mount

Lebanon. As he wrote, rather triumphantly, to the London Society:

Lady Hester Stanhope, well-known as the niece, confidant and domestic manager of a departed Premier in England, a lady of no ordinary talent, research and enterprise, has opened her house to me. I am going to repose under her roof till I can occupy a place she has taken for me on the top of Mount Lebanon where we can employ the summer in preparing for the future by the study of language and the formation of the habits necessary to an Arab life. The place is eminently suited to the reception of Missionaries on their arrival to learn Arabic and Syrian and other things equally necessary.[14]

Once again, Way had found the right patron. Lady Hester, with her prestige and knowledge of the Near East, seemed the ideal person to find the site for, and help establish, the missionary college. More exciting still, there appeared to be a general sense throughout the region that the Millennium was imminent. As Way put it in a letter to Mary:

Lady Hester . . . has travelled all over the land from Palmyra to Cairo, is acquainted with the politics, character and history, public and private, of all parties in the land, and having gained the confidence of the knowing part of the community, she is able to testify to their general expectations, which are that the Ottoman Empire will soon fall, that these countries will be separated from it, that great troubles will soon commence in every part of Europe . . . and that, above all, the Elect or Enlightened will soon flock to these parts in expectation of the great Deliverer, whom some call the Haken, some the Mahdi, some the Messiah and we the Christ: that he will execute the last judgements on the wicked by famine, pestilence, battle, murder and sudden death, during which the Just will be preserved and finally established here on the restoration of the Jews and the appearance of the Ancient Prophets. This most extraordinary coincidence with what you know to be my most decided and sure hope is the more remarkable as it is chiefly deduced from communications with Jews, Arabs, Persians, and Oriental Books; of which some are yet said to be in the possession of Eastern Jews and Magi . . . Lady Hester is preparing herself for these events.[15]

Inevitably, Lady Hester's eccentric lifestyle had led to speculation about her sanity. Way was aware of this, but meeting her and listening to her discourses soon dispelled his own doubts on that score. Lady Hester had an incredibly sharp mind and a delivery as brilliant as her uncle's. Unfortunately for Way, this delivery was interminable. As her English physician, Dr Charles Meryon, put it after her death, in his three-volume *Memoirs of the Lady Hester Stanhope*:

Her marked characteristic was the necessity of eternally talking, a feature of her life which can hardly be done justice to by description. Her brain worked incessantly and her tongue never knew a moment's repose. Her conversations lasted eight and ten hours at a time, without moving from her seat; she seemed entirely to forget that the listener could possibly require a respite . . . Lady Hester herself told me that Mr. Lewis Way remained one day from three in the afternoon till break of day next morning tête-à-tête with her.[16]

Fortunately, Lady Hester had presented Way with a fine Arab mare on which he was able temporarily to escape. In the course of various local expeditions, he and Albert had found an abandoned Jesuit College at Antoura, a beautiful but remote spot. Way thought it the perfect place to establish the Jewish Mission. As he later recalled: 'Many were the hopes I encouraged, the plans I formed, and the prayers I poured forth for future usefulness on this spot.'[17]

Just as this cherished dream seemed about to be realised, Way was suddenly struck down. An inflammatory eruption in his legs turned quickly into a dangerous fever. Albert decided it was vital to get his father back to France for medical treatment, but he was too sick to be moved. Way suffered the heat of July before he could be moved to the coast where they boarded a ship sailing for Genoa. Mr Lewis was left behind to arrange the missionary college and retain the useful, if exhausting, connection with Lady Hester. With the journey to Jerusalem abandoned, Way realised that, like Moses, he would never see the Holy Land.

Lewis and Albert Way endured a terrible voyage before the ship eventually docked at Leghorn. As the plague was still raging in Syria, they and the rest of the passengers were kept in quarantine, but Lewis and Albert Way at least had the consolation of being reunited with some of their family – though at a healthy distance. Now aged fifty-one, having spent the previous twelve years pursuing his mission and undertaking long and exhausting journeys, Way was in poor health. Yet within six weeks he was not only back on his feet, but back on his horse. The Arab mare that Lady Hester had given him had survived the horrific voyage. The family's destination was Nice, and, not surprisingly, Way had no desire for another sea journey. He opted to go on horseback from Genoa to Nice, a distance of 120 miles, with Drusilla, now twenty, and Aunt Kitty, who was forty-one. On the switchback route along the coast they at least had the consolation of a back-up coach if exhaustion or storms set in. Meanwhile Mary and the children had a storm-tossed voyage that took them almost as long. As a family, the Ways were not fortunate with the Mediterranean.

While Way was completing his recuperation in Nice, he received a huge blow to both his pride and his loyalty to the London Society. In his absence it had published the tract, *Thoughts on the Scriptural Expectations of the Christian Church*, that he had written under the name Basilicus almost a year before. This dealt in part with Way's violently apocalyptic view of the Millennium. The prevailing doctrine of the Church of England did not place great emphasis on the Millennium, viewing it as a distant prospect, and presenting its nature as essentially peaceful. Yet Way, cleaving to his literalist interpretation of the Book of Revelation, argued that the Second Coming preceding the Millennium, and the Last Judgement succeeding it, would be bloody and cataclysmic events. They would involve earth-shaking battles and the wholesale punishment of sinners before the restoration of the Jews and the final overthrow of Satan. He was also convinced that they were imminent. As he expressed it in the pamphlet:

Doubtless the days are *fulfilled*, when Christians should be warned to flee from the wrath to come . . . when earnest supplication should be made for the restoration of Israel, and when the beginning of sorrows, and judgements on the professing house of God, call loudly on his people to escape out of Babylon, lest they partake of her plagues, and sink in her fall.[18]

The pamphlet led to numerous acrimonious protests from the Society's membership, the more knowledgeable of them realising, uncomfortably, that Basilicus was their own great benefactor and vice-president. The controversy exposed the division inherent in the London Society since its foundation, between those who pursued the conversion of the Jews simply as a good in itself, and the millenarians who did so with their eyes fixed on the prophecies of Revelation. For the moment, the former were in the ascendant, and they felt that Basilicus' bloodcurdling predictions might well alienate new or potential converts.

It remains one of the mysteries of Way's character that a man of such gentleness and charm, who in his daily life showed compassion to all, should have held such apocalyptic beliefs that entailed the slaughter of millions. Amazingly he somehow managed to reconcile these beliefs with his everyday behaviour. In fact, what distinguished him from other missionaries and visionaries, and brought him greater success, was that these unbudgeable views hid behind the façade of a benign and highly cultivated English gentleman.

To resolve this dispute, Sir Thomas Baring, the president of the Society, wrote to Way as persuasively and diplomatically as he could, asking him if he would refrain from propagating his views in print. From Paris, Way replied:

Your letter found me in perfect peace and disturbed me not. Having been in peril on the sea, in peril of robbers, in journeying often, in weariness and painfulness, literally in hunger and thirst, in labour abundant nigh unto death, it is perhaps only another and useful trial that I should be in peril by mine own countrymen or in peril among false brethren. I can only say that when during a night and day I was on the deep, driven by a storm from Malta, I expected either to go to the bottom, or to be sent home in one of my long boxes to Stansted, yet I had no misgivings or repentings in regard to Basilican notions.[19]

Way also wrote separately to Baring as a friend, 'Is it true that you wish and even enjoin that the Personal Advent (whether Millennium be added or not is no matter) should be kept out of sight as much as possible?' When Baring wrote back and said that, sadly, under the circumstances, this was true, Way resigned his vice-presidency. Even Mary and his two older children were against his decision, feeling it would leave him isolated from his mission, but Way was adamant. His view of the Last Days allowed of no compromise. If the Book of Revelation said there would be two Armageddons there would be two.

Lewis Way's spirits and his mission never totally recovered from his split with the London Society. His friends urged him to return to England and attend its next meeting, in the hope that a way forward could be found, but he refused, fearing that any sort of confrontation might actually kill him:

I entreat you for God's sake, and for the Cause sake, and for my life's sake (if that were of any consequence), think not of my coming to your meeting . . . Your Society has had my time and property and undivided attention for upwards of 12 years . . .You have no right to take my life which would certainly be endangered by my coming over now . . .[20]

Way and his family stayed on in Paris where, despite an increasing shortage of money, they led a full and expensive social life. Years later Drusilla reminisced in her journal:

I remember going to the Ambassador's reception; crowds of élite, male and female, I holding fast to the Paternal arm, he nudged me and said 'Talleyrand', and there he was, lame, but with a head like Saul, above all the rest, and a peculiar one.[21]

As for Way's financial problems, a solution was at hand – lightning struck twice. This time it was Mary's aunt who died, leaving her a considerable property in England, a residual sum of £25,000 (approx £1.8 million at today's value) as well as separate legacies to her husband and Drusilla. It was not as great a fortune as John Way had left twenty years before, but it did guarantee the family a life of permanent ease and it didn't take Way long to find a

Coming home: the cross-Channel packet.
Drawing by Albert Way.

philanthropic use for some of it. He had discovered that there were upwards of 1,500 British residents in Paris but no Anglican church for them to worship in. A weekly service was held in a room at the Embassy which could hold only 200.

Way then discovered that the Hotel Marboeuf nearby was for sale. Part of it could easily be converted into a chapel and the rest would make a fine residence for himself and his family. He negotiated to buy the property, only to discover that he would need royal permission to proceed and that the King was anxious not to give offence to the Jesuits by opening an Anglican church in the centre of Paris. Way then had a meeting with Louis XVIII's prime minister, the Comte de Villèle, who advised it might only be possible if George IV wrote a letter to the French King asking for it as a personal favour. Fortunately Way still had connections in court circles and the two kings exchanged letters. By mid-1824 the church was completed and functioning. That Christmas, Lady Granville, the wife of the ambassador, wrote to her sister: 'I went this morning to hear Lewis Way preach. His sermons are extemporary; he is evangelical and very striking and impressive. The English flock there. If anyone whispers, he stops and says: "When Lady Such-and-Such has done talking I will proceed."'[22]

With his other project, the one nearest his heart – turning Stansted into a Missionary College – his influence in high places had been less successful. Way and the family returned to Stansted in 1825 and he made a final effort to influence the government in his favour. He appealed again to his friend Lord Liverpool, the prime minister, to influence the King and Privy Council on his behalf. The King, having already pleaded Way's cause as regards the conversion of the Hotel Marboeuf, was not prepared to be as helpful with the conversion of the Jews. In royal and government circles the idea of proselytising was no longer fashionable. Way had finally to accept that there would be no official charter for Stansted as a missionary college. If so, was there now any point in the huge expense of maintaining the house and its large estate? Again he turned to his friends for advice. They all agreed that Stansted should be sold.

Way was further depressed by the news that in December his once most powerful friend, Czar Alexander, had died in Moscow, at the age of forty-eight, without having fulfilled any of the projects, which he and Way had discussed so intensely. His brother, Nicholas I, who succeeded him, was to introduce a policy of Jewish assimilation based on repression. The three million Russian and Polish Jews were never to know what a champion they had had in Lewis Way, and he was never to know of the entirely different form of Zionism that would eventually take root among them.

At the age of fifty-three, after twelve years of unremitting work and travel, Way's life's mission appeared to have come to a discouraging end. His fortune and energies may have been depleted, but he never gave up his belief in the imminence of a Second Coming and the final acceptance by the Jews of the true saviour. Now he had to accept it would come only by divine intervention unaided by any human endeavour. In 1826 Stansted was sold and Way returned with his family to Paris. They took up residence in the Hotel Marboeuf and Way returned to his priestly duties in the adjoining chapel, his sermons drawing large and fashionable crowds. Reflecting in the tranquillity of her journal, many years later, Drusilla wrote: 'And all success followed the merciful difficulties against a Stansted Jewish College, which would have ruined us all, and probably failed of success entirely.'[23]

Although Stansted had been sold, a neighbouring country house provided the setting for Lewis Way's last major contribution to Christian Zionism. In the wake of his dispute with the London Society, Way and an influential group of millenarians, including the banker and MP Henry Drummond and the fashionable preacher Edward Irving, formed the Society for the Investigation of Prophecy. In November 1826, it held its first conference at Drummond's home, Albury Park in Hampshire. Among the forty participants who joined Way there were the famous traveller and converted Jew, Joseph Wolff, and the biblical commentator James Hatley Frere. The main topics discussed were all central to Way's concerns, especially the signs of the approaching Millennium and the restoration of the Jews. Eventually, after five annual conferences, the group broke up. It was, however, to form one of Way's most enduring legacies to the present day, though in a manner he could never have anticipated.

In 1829 Way's health deteriorated. He found and paid for a replacement minister at Marboeuf while he sought a cure at one of the numerous spas that were currently in vogue. He started at Aix-les-Bains and then went on to Bath, neither proving particularly beneficial. He then heard of the enormous reputation of a Dr Jephson and his Walking Cure at Leamington Spa.[24] Way enrolled himself there. Whatever effect this treatment had on him, it certainly didn't affect his wit. In reply to a friend who asked him about Jephson's regime, he wrote a poem entitled *Leamington Peripatetics*:

> He does, Sir, for all those who Jephson obey,
> Walk out in all seasons, all hours of the day.
> They walk when the North wind blows piercing and bleak
> They walk when their mouths are so stiff they can't speak:
> They walk in the mists and cold fogs of November
> They walk in the drizzle and damp of December.
> They walk when it thaws and they walk when it freezes,
> They walk for all causes, to cure all diseases . . .

The plethoric walk to make them grow paler
The pallid ones walk to make them grow haler.
The stout and unwieldy they're walking for that
The bony and skinny walk to grow fat.
If some walk too slowly they're joined by the Master
Then, surprising to see, they walk faster and faster!
In short, he makes those walk who ne'er walked before,
And those who have always walked, here still more . . .[25]

There are several more stanzas, though they do not record what effect the Jephson Cure had on Way. Its memories clearly did not daunt him, as he subsequently bought a house in Leamington and lived there with his family for the last ten years of his life. He died peacefully on 23 January 1840, and was buried in All Saints' Church.[26]

Drusilla never married but became the keeper of the paternal flame, preserving many of his writings and letters. She continued to live in Leamington. From there, on the 18 July 1873, she wrote to a great-niece who had been staying at Wonham, the house of Lewis Way's son Albert, where he kept his father's account of his interviews with Alexander I:

I fear you did not see the 'Interviews' at Wonham. They are the cream of all the old documents, and every Way descendant ought to read them as well as to have their minds alive to Jewish Interests. I have often regretted that it should not come more hitherto before you dear young people. Would that I had strength to tell you more about the interest, and what a brilliant attraction there was in your dear grandfather

– how noble his mind, how sparkling his wit, how spiritual his thoughts, how deep his love to rich and poor in whom he felt there was the love divine, from a Czar to a beggar. But on these things I cannot dwell.[27]

~

Lewis Way never returned to Miss Parminter's oaks at *à la Ronde*, the source that had inspired his life-time mission on that winter morning in 1811. In the summer of 1882, forty-two years after Way's death, Benjamin Bradley, the accountant of the London Society, was on his summer holidays in Devon and decided he would like to see *à la Ronde* for himself. The story of Miss Parminter's codicil and Way's con-versionary experience were well known to him, as it would have been to all members of the Society. Endless talks had been given and numerous pam-phlets written about it. It was, after all, only Way's generosity that had enabled the Society to survive and spread its mission.

Having inspected the famous oaks for himself, Bradley decided to pursue his researches further and look up the inspirational codicil about 'the hand of man not being raised against them until Is-rael returns and is restored to the Land of Promise'. To his great surprise and disappointment Bradley discovered that no such codicil existed. Locally it had been well known that Jane Parminter had a predilection for the Jewish people. She may well have said something about their destined fate that fuelled the legend, but there was no reference to any oaks in any will left by her. Back in London, Bradley felt obliged to report his discovery. The Society was severely embarrassed and immediately withdrew all its literature on the subject.[28] The legend of the oaks and the effect it had on Lewis Way was never referred to again. Yet if his inspiration was based on a myth, his own integrity was never questioned, and his work and influence on Christian Zionism by no means ended with his death.

– Epilogue –

Lewis Way never achieved his 'Point in View' in his lifetime and, barring the actual Second Coming, his dream of a mass conversion of the Jews to Christianity seems as far off as ever. Yet the mission that Miss Parminter's oaks inspired did not end entirely in failure. The other half of Way's dream – the restoration of the Jews to the Holy Land – did happen, and was achieved after events between 1939 and 1945 that fulfilled the most violent and apocalyptic visions of his Basilicus.

Like his benefactor John Way, Lewis Way left an enormous legacy. To modern Zionism it was two-fold. The first helped bring about the Balfour Declaration and the creation of the Jewish homeland. The second has provided a powerful support for the State of Israel to the present day. Way's first legacy was essentially British; his second took root and achieved a remarkable growth in America.

In Britain, Way's posthumous contribution to Zionism came through the London Society that he had rescued almost single-handedly in 1815, and for which he had laboured so devotedly. On two occasions before the First World War, the London Society, and influential individuals connected with it, made serious attempts to restore the Jews to the Holy Land. They did so by the method Way had so successfully demonstrated with Czar Alexander of Russia – gaining the backing of a great power for a Jewish homeland through the careful cultivation of its ruler. Significantly, by the end of the nineteenth century these Christian Zionists were increasingly acting in collaboration with Jewish Zionists.

Their first attempt came very close to success and, in retrospect, was a dress rehearsal for the Balfour Declaration. It took place in the summer of 1840, ironically just six months after Lewis Way's death. It involved several of his former collaborators, principally his prize recruit Alexander McCaul, and Sir Thomas Baring, who had become president of the London Society at Way's urging. Its guiding spirit though was Lord Ashley (to become Earl of Shaftesbury in 1851), the most politically powerful Evangelical of his day and, after 1848, Baring's successor as President of the London Society. Outwardly forbidding, Ashley was equipped with great intellect and energy. Today he is best remembered for his contribution to social reform in Britain, especially to the Factory Acts and the Ragged Schools. All of his campaigns, however, were motivated by a profound belief in humanity's need to prepare for the Second Coming, and in this, of course, the conversion and restoration of the Jews played a critical role.[1]

Like Lewis Way twenty years earlier, Ashley's greatest asset for the Christian Zionists was his excellent access to the corridors of power, and especially to his stepfather-in-law, the leading politician Lord Palmerston, who became foreign secretary in 1835. From then on, what could be seen as a 'Christian lobby' brought its influence to bear on Palmerston to help the Jews achieve a homeland. Palmerston was emphatically not a religious man, but quickly realised the possibilities that protecting the Jews in the Ottoman empire offered for the extension of British power in the Middle East. In this way, Ashley helped persuade Palmerston late in 1838 to appoint a British vice-consul in Jerusalem, with responsibility for all of Palestine 'within its ancient limits' and a particular duty 'to afford protection to the Jews generally'. Significantly, the London Society elected the new vice-consul, William Young, to its general committee just before his departure.[2]

At the same time Ashley, closely seconded by McCaul, championed a related project: the building of a church in Jerusalem, 'Protestant in content, Hebrew in form',[3] to spread the word of the Gospel among the Jews of Palestine. This held a strong echo of Lewis Way's effort to establish the missionary college on Mount Lebanon. Once more Palmerston lent his good offices, but the scheme languished till championed by another of the highly placed friends that Way had made on his travels, the Crown Prince of Prussia, now King Frederick William IV. The result was remarkable – a joint Anglican-Lutheran Bishopric of Jerusalem, funded equally by Britain and Prussia. McCaul was offered the See, but felt it should go instead to a converted Jew, the rabbinical scholar M. S. Alexander. When Alexander accepted, McCaul stepped into his shoes as Professor of Hebrew at King's College London, a post he held until the end of his life.[4]

Ashley, McCaul and their collaborators explicitly viewed the vice-consulate and the Bishopric of Jerusalem as practical steps towards their overall scheme for the conversion and final restoration of the Jews. When Young was appointed vice-consul, Ashley commented: 'He is . . . accredited, as it were, to the former Kingdom of David and the Twelve Tribes.' In a long article in the *Quarterly Review* of January 1839, Ashley envisaged the prospect of British protection inducing the Jews to flock to the Holy Land in large numbers 'and become once more the husbandmen of Judea and Galilee'.[5] Lewis Way had always realised the necessity for a great power to underwrite the return of the Jews to Palestine, but for him this had been Alexander I's Russia. Now Britain took on this role, and did not relinquish it till 1948.

For Way's and Ashley's vision to have any reality, the situation in the Middle East needed to change dramatically. In 1840, it did exactly that. For several years, the Ottoman Sultan had been at loggerheads with an over-mighty subject, the Viceroy of Egypt Mehmet Ali, who wished to add Syria (which then included Palestine) to his domains. In pursuit of this goal, Mehmet Ali won a series of military victories over the Sultan that brought the Ottoman empire to its knees. The result was a major international crisis; France supported Mehmet Ali's claims, but Britain, Austria and Russia, fearing the international consequences of the Turkish empire unravelling too soon and too completely, backed the Sultan. On 15 July 1840, these three powers issued an ultimatum to Mehmet Ali to evacuate his Syrian conquests or face armed intervention. For the next few months it seemed as if Mehmet Ali, in alliance with France, would refuse, that the Ottoman empire would collapse, and that this would precipitate a general European war.[6]

Lord Ashley immediately seized his chance to fish in these troubled waters. On 1 August he dined with Palmerston and set before him a remarkable scheme. In order to pacify and develop the areas currently under dispute, Ashley argued that the Jews should be encouraged to return to their ancient homeland. The Sultan should be prevailed upon to issue an edict promising security of life and property to all immigrant Jews, under the guarantee of the European, and particularly the British, consular representatives. Ashley shrewdly downplayed the underlying millenarian aim of the project, since he knew this would alarm his worldly stepfather-in-law. As he confided to his diary: 'I am forced to argue politically, financially, commercially; these considerations strike home.'[7]

Ashley's tactics worked; his arguments excited Palmerston, who promised to further the scheme. As good as his word, ten days later he sent a despatch to the British Ambassador in Constantinople, instructing him to urge 'the Turkish government . . . to hold out every just encouragement to the Jews of Europe to return to Palestine', and citing all the reasons Ashley had just given him. Palmerston also launched a press campaign to promote the project and test public opinion.[8] On 17 August *The Times* published a sympathetic leading article, recommending all enlightened statesmen 'to consider whether this remarkable people . . . under national institutions might not be advantageously employed for the interests of civilization in the East.'

These were heady days for the Christian Zionists; for a few months it seemed as if the historic restoration of the Jews might finally be achieved. This was to reckon without the guile and basic hostility of the Sultan. By the end of 1840, Britain and her allies had delivered him from the threat of Mehmet Ali, and with this menace removed he no longer had any need to please Palmerston. Like Lewis Way after Aix-la-Chapelle, Lord Ashley found that official support for his scheme quickly dissolved as the international situation changed. Yet his achievement should not be underestimated. At a moment when the Ottoman empire seemed about to collapse, a concrete plan for settling Jews in Palestine had been proposed and had won the backing of a British foreign secretary. Seventy-seven years later history repeated itself, only this time the Ottoman empire did collapse, and a Jewish homeland became a reality.

Despite this failure in 1840, Ashley still had two more contributions to make to the cause. In 1853 he wrote memorably that Palestine, 'a country without a nation', was the obvious home for 'a nation without a country'. Fifty years later, the novelist Israel Zangwill adapted the phrase to create Jewish Zionism's most effective slogan: 'A country without a people for a people without a country.'[9]

Succeeding his father as Earl of Shaftesbury in 1851, Ashley continued his close involvement with Christian Zionism, particularly with the fortunes of the Bishopric of Jerusalem. However, his last intervention in Jewish affairs, just three years before his death, was strictly humanitarian rather than Messianic. In 1881, a wave of pogroms convulsed Russian Jewry, causing death, dislocation, and a tide of emigration. In early 1882, Shaftesbury organised and addressed a mass meeting at the Mansion House to protest to the Russian government and mobilise efforts to relieve Jewish suffering. His speech inspired a young clergyman, William Hechler, who was in the audience. Hechler was the son of a German London Society missionary and an English mother. He was himself an active member of the Society and immediately volunteered to spent the next year in the Ukraine, working on behalf of Shaftesbury's Jewish Relief Committee with homeless refugees. A committed millenarian and restorationist, Hechler was struck by how many of these victims saw a return to Palestine as their only hope. He devoted the rest of his life to making this a reality – Shaftesbury's acolyte became his successor.[10]

Unlike Lewis Way and Shaftesbury, Hechler had no private income, so his mission was often subordinated to the necessity of making a living. He was a brilliant scholar and linguist and, through a well-connected godmother, he became tutor to the sons of the Grand Duke of Baden, and then chaplain to the British embassy in Vienna. It was here, due to him, that British Christian Zionism made a radical departure from its roots. In February 1896, Hechler read Theodor Herzl's pamphlet *Der Judenstaat.* He knew that Herzl was an editor at the *Neue Freie Presse,* whose offices were nearby. Hechler quickly arranged a meeting with him there, and pledged to help him create a Jewish state.[11] This impulsive action set in motion a crucial process. From an evangelising, conversionist movement, Christian Zionism increasingly became the handmaiden to Jewish Zionism, and has remained so to the present day.

Since Herzl was clearly not about to convert to Christianity, an obvious question arises. Jewish Zionism would certainly advance the restoration of the Jews, but definitely not their conversion. Hechler's solution to this conundrum was eminently practical. The essential aim was to open the doors of Palestine to the Jews – once there their conversion could be left to God's will as set out in the Book of Revelation. As Hechler expressed it to a missionary friend in 1898:

Of course you look for the conversion of the Jews, but the times are changing rapidly, and it is important for us to look further and higher. We are now entering, thanks to the Zionist movement, into Israel's Messianic age. Thus, it is not a matter these days of opening all the doors of your churches to the Jew, but rather of opening the gates to their homeland . . .[12]

Hechler's words became the principle of most subsequent Christian Zionist organisations, particularly in America, where they experienced their most spectacular growth. Unlike the London Society of Lewis Way's time, these groups have downplayed their conversionist beliefs and stressed instead their unwavering support for a Jewish homeland and, after 1948, for the state of Israel, and its expansion to its ancient biblical limits.

Though Hechler lacked Lewis Way's and Shaftesbury's connections, he certainly had their talent for gaining access to the corridors of power. It was here he proved most useful to Herzl. Through his former employer the Grand Duke of Baden, who conveniently also happened to be a Christian Zionist, Hechler brought Herzl into contact with the Grand Duke's nephew, Kaiser Wilhelm II. This was an extremely shrewd move, for not only was Germany cultivating close ties with the Ottoman empire, but the Kaiser himself was about to make a trip to the Holy Land, passing through Constantinople en route. If he would agree to persuade the Sultan into opening Palestine to Jewish settlement, Herzl's goal would come very much closer.

On 20 October 1898, Herzl had an interview with the Kaiser in Constantinople. With the way prepared by his uncle, Wilhelm promised Herzl he would speak to the Sultan in his favour. He also suggested a symbolic meeting with Herzl in the Holy Land itself. On 28 October, accompanied by Hechler, Herzl greeted the Kaiser at the gate of Mikveh Israel, the first Jewish agricultural school established in Palestine, near present-day Tel Aviv. In the interim Wilhelm had spoken to the Sultan and discovered his complete hostility to the Zionist plan. The encounter at Mikveh Israel was thus brief and disappointing. Even the photographer on hand to record the moment botched his job. Although Herzl was standing next to the mounted Kaiser, only his foot appeared in the picture, which had to be doctored later to add the rest of his body.[13]

Through all the vicissitudes of Herzl's campaign, Hechler remained his faithful friend and ally. He was one of only three Christian Zionist delegates to the First Zionist Congress of 1897 at Basel, and when Herzl turned from Germany to Britain as a potential backer for Zionism, he did his best to mobilise his contacts there to support him. Worn out by overwork and travel, Herzl died in 1904 at the age of only forty-four. It was Hechler who was by his side to record his last words – 'Greet Palestine for me. I gave my heart's blood for my people.'[14] Hechler survived his friend by many years, though in increasingly straitened circumstances, living mainly on a pension of £10 a month from Zionist organisations. In the last years of his life, Hechler, frequently prone to prophesying, repeatedly warned his Jewish friends that there would soon be large-scale massacres of Jews in Europe. He died aged eighty-five in the public ward of the London Hospital in 1931.[15]

By then the fulfilment of the Balfour Declaration had established a Jewish homeland – of sorts – in Palestine. In this endeavour, for the first time, Christian Zionism played only a secondary role. Herzl's successor as leader of the Zionist movement, Chaim Weizmann, a brilliant Russian émigré chemist teaching at Manchester University, used the technique, pioneered by Lewis Way, Shaftesbury and Hechler, of acquiring powerful patrons. He did this directly with no Christian intermediaries, and does not, for example, seem to have had any contact with Hechler personally. Weizmann had met and first discussed Zionism in 1906 with the Conservative politician Arthur Balfour, who had been much impressed with his intellect and charm. Ten years later, in the midst of the First World War, the conversation was resumed. By then Weizmann's research had made a considerable contribution to the British war effort and Balfour was foreign secretary in Lloyd George's coalition government. The situation was now entirely different. The Ottoman empire, having taken Germany's side in the war, was destined to be dismantled in the event of an Allied victory. Weizmann and Balfour collaborated to ensure that the planned new order in the Middle East would include a Jewish homeland. This decision was made public in the Balfour Declaration of 2 November 1917.[16]

Balfour and Lloyd George, who approved his actions, were certainly not Christian Zionists in the mould of Lewis Way and Shaftesbury, and certainly did not share their millenarian beliefs. Yet both men had had deeply Protestant upbringings, and were steeped in the Old Testament – Lloyd George later recalled that during his first discussion with Weizmann about Palestine in December 1914, place names kept coming into the conversation that were more familiar to him than those of the Western Front.[17] In addition, the humanitarian efforts of Way, Shaftesbury and the London Society on behalf of the Jews over the last century had played their part. These had created a current of sympathy for them in British literature and culture that ultimately had an effect on policy-makers. Balfour himself was fond of repeating that 'Christian religion and civilization owes to Judaism an immeasurable debt, shamefully ill repaid.'[18]

Though it had played no direct role in the genesis of the Balfour Declaration, the London Society, in its journal, *The Jewish Expositor*, swiftly published a statement welcoming the Declaration, and placing it firmly in the context of biblical prophecy:

With one step the Jewish cause has made a great bound forward . . . What does all this mean for us Christians? In the light of prophetic Scripture we recognize that such an action on the part of the Allied Powers . . . is full of significance . . . now we seem to be on the very verge of a literal fulfilment of the last prediction, and it is certainly a distinct warning to us that the Lord 'is near, even at the very doors'.[19]

These were of course the views of a minority, but one event in the final year of the war must have given even cynics a twinge of foreboding. Nine months after General Allenby entered Jerusalem at the head of a British army in December 1917, he defeated the last Turkish forces in the Holy Land at Megiddo – the biblical site of Armageddon. When elevated to the peerage in 1919, in an incongruous juxtaposition of the apocalyptic and the provincial, he took the title of Viscount Allenby of Megiddo and Felixstowe.

The Balfour Declaration and the establishment of the Palestine Mandate marked the high point of British support for Zionism. In the following decades this markedly cooled, as the new overlords of the Holy Land struggled fruitlessly to reconcile the competing claims of Jew and Arab. By 1948 the Mandate had become a burden which Britain was only too happy to lay down. The State of Israel was born, and increasingly turned to a new great power as protector, the USA. The bond between America and Israel has now grown to almost unbreakable strength, and forms the basis of Israel's security, politically and militarily. Much of this reflects American strategic considerations, but also the presence of a large Jewish population in the country itself, and sympathy for the Jews in the wake of the Holocaust. Yet Christian Zionism also played a significant part, and it is here that Lewis Way's last legacy still survives.

The origins of American Christian Zionism lie in Britain, in the work of Lewis Way and his colleagues in the last decades of his life. They can be traced specifically to those Albury Park conferences, convened after Way's suggestion to his friend Henry Drummond that they bring together a group of eminent figures 'without distinction of sect or party' who held to 'the Jewish and Christian hope'.[20] One important participant in the conference was Theodosia, Lady Powerscourt, the beautiful and pious widow of an Irish peer, and a passionate Evangelical and millenarian. When the Albury Park conferences ended in 1830, she carried on their tradition without a break by hosting an annual conference of her own at Powerscourt Castle near Dublin. It is not clear whether Way was there, but John Nelson Darby certainly was. He was the man who did most to build on Way's ideas and, crucially, to export them to the USA.

Born in 1800, Darby was a Church of Ireland clergyman who had resigned his curacy in 1828 to become a full-time missionary.[21] Unimpressive in appearance and not an obviously charismatic preacher, he had enormous powers of intellect and persuasion. A strong biblical literalist and believer in an imminent Second Coming, Darby had closely followed the proceedings at the Albury Park conferences and was soon the star of the Powerscourt gatherings. As at Albury Park, the Jews and their role in the Millennium formed a major theme of the discussions. At the second conference, one of the questions debated was: 'By what covenant did the Jews, and shall the Jews, hold the land?'[22]

Darby's first major contribution to Christian Zionism was theological. He pioneered the doctrine of Dispensationalism, which divided all of human history, on a religious basis, into successive 'dispensations'. For Darby, the current dispensation, that of the Christian Church, was nearing its end, and would soon be replaced by the Messianic age. Above all, he formulated the concept of the Rapture. Just before the Second Coming, Christ would descend briefly to earth and sweep up all true believers to Heaven, thus sparing them the horrors of Armageddon. At a stroke, the unappealing prospect of blood and fire that Lewis Way had envisaged, and for which even the London Society had had little enthusiasm, was replaced by a much more reassuring vision. Now the faithful would watch from above while most of humanity (including those Jews who had not accepted Christ) perished. As Lady Powerscourt picturesquely put it, 'our heaven will be in a cloud, suspended over the New Jerusalem'.[23]

The Rapture, of course, was far more likely to attract converts than Lewis Way's altogether grimmer vision. And make converts it did, particularly when Darby took his message to America in a series of evangelising tours between 1862 and 1877. Darby himself was more a writer than a speaker, but his successors, men like Dwight L. Moody and Cyrus I. Schofield, were great orators, and created a huge following for the theology formulated by Darby. The Rapture remains today one of the key beliefs of conservative American Evangelicalism.[24]

If Darby's doctrines were more enticing than those set out by Way in the 1820s, the conversion and restoration of the Jews remained at their core. As had happened in Britain, the American version increasingly downplayed conversion, leaving it to God's good offices rather than to human agency. It emphasised instead the return of the Jews to the Promised Land. This ensured that the creation of Israel in 1948 was welcomed by American Evangelists: two of its most prominent leaders, the Rev. Jerry Falwell and Pastor John Hagee, have separately recalled how the event inspired them.[25]

The complex story that links Lewis Way to the American religious right and to Israel has one further twist. In the 1970s, in response to what it saw as the growing permissiveness, liberalism and secularisation of America, US Evangelicalism mobilised as a political force on a greater scale than ever before. The result was Jerry Falwell's Moral Majority, and then its successor, Pat Robertson's Christian Coalition. The use of television to spread the message, raise funds and fill the vast new mega-churches played a major part in this expansion. While the main concerns of these groups were domestic, they also had strong views on foreign policy. The Christian Zionism, to which so many of them adhered, dictated unwavering support for Israel. As Jerry Falwell said: 'You can't belong to Moral Majority without being a Zionist.'[26]

Israeli politicians on the right soon spotted the immense advantages that collaboration with the

American religious right could bring. The first to do so was Menachem Begin. Brushing aside theological differences, he realised how much influence such a large religious lobby could have on the world's greatest superpower. The figures bore him out: in Gallup polls carried out from 1976 to 2001, between 33 and 47 per cent of Americans described themselves as Evangelical or 'Born-Again'. Though not all of these were necessarily Christian Zionists, a large percentage were.[27]

Since the 1970s, the American religious right has been an essential ally of the Israeli right, most recently in the Middle East peace process. It opposed the Oslo accords of 1993 which paved the way for a Palestinian state, and has consistently campaigned against any surrender of the biblical land of Israel, which includes Judea and Samaria. Further proof of its support for the Israeli right came in January 1998. The Israeli Prime Minister, Binyamin Netanyahu, who opposed the Oslo accords, flew to Washington for a difficult meeting with their sponsor, President Clinton. Yet instead of going first to the White House he went to the Mayflower Hotel, to a meeting of one thousand leading Christian Zionists organised by Jerry Falwell. Fortified by their loud support, at his meeting next day with President Clinton he stuck to the stonewalling policy that has helped to make peace in the Middle East so elusive to this day.[28]

Under Clinton's successor, the born-again George W. Bush, the influence of the religious right became even more pronounced. In March 2002, after a suicide bombing in Netanya during the Second Intifada, the Israeli army attacked the Palestinian town of Jenin on the West Bank. After an international outcry President Bush was persuaded to send a message to Prime Minister Sharon to withdraw. Meanwhile Falwell and the other Christian Zionist leaders mobilised their constituency, which flooded the White House with emails and letters and jammed the telephone switchboard. After that, President Bush never again pronounced against Israeli policy or actions, and Falwell was able to tell large television audiences that President Bush would 'do the right thing for Israel every time' and that 'the Bible Belt is Israel's safety net in the US'.[29]

More recently, Binyamin Netanyahu, once again Israeli prime minister, has shown himself adept at judging how to get round political pressure from the US. In order to gain concessions in the Palestinian-Israeli peace negotiations in September and October 2010, Barack Obama tried to persuade Netanyahu to extend the moratorium on settlement building on the West Bank and in East Jerusalem. The timing perfectly suited Netanyahu, not Obama. With the US mid-term Congressional elections taking place in early November no president would endanger his party's chances by leaning too heavily on Israel and provoking both the Christian and the Jewish Zionists in the country. Netanyahu could comfortably remain obdurate.

What, one wonders, would Lewis Way make of the actual outcome of his efforts for the restoration of the Jews? The early twenty-first century is separated from the early nineteenth by upheavals that would have beggared even his vivid imagination. Antichrists and Armageddons have come and gone, peace treaties have been signed and torn up. Yet it is striking how far the two aspects of Way's legacy, the British and the American, still reflect the different sides of his own divided personality. Would he have recognised himself in the intellectual and urbane Arthur Balfour, or in the fire-and-brimstone fundamentalist Jerry Falwell? One can only set out the remarkable and neglected story of his journey, respect the generosity of his intentions, and echo the hope expressed in one of his hymns to Zion:

> No more shall violence and war
> Thy sure foundations raze;
> For, lo! Thy walls salvation are,
> Thy gates eternal praise!

– Notes –

Introduction

1 For the American religious right and the Moral Majority,
the best introductions are W. H. Capps, *The New Religious
Right: Piety, Patriotism and Politics* (Columbia, SC, 1990); D.
D'Sousa, *Falwell: Before the Millennium* (Chicago, 1984); J.
C. Green, M. J. Rozell and C. Wilcox, *The Christian Right in
American Politics: Marching to the Millennium* (Washington,
DC, 2003); S. F. Harding, *The Book of Jerry Falwell:
Fundamentalist Language and Politics* (Princeton, NJ, 2000);
and E. Kaplan, *With God on their Side: George W. Bush and
the Christian Right* (New York, 2004).

2 See, *inter alia*, V. Clark, *Allies for Armageddon: The Rise
of Christian Zionism* (New Haven and London, 2007),
pp.190–2, and S. Spector, *Evangelicals and Israel: The Story
of American Christian Zionism* (Oxford, 2009), pp.142–4,
147–8.

3 Cited in P. R. Wilkinson, *For Zion's Sake: Christian Zionism
and the Role of John Nelson Darby* (Milton Keynes, 2007),
p.221.

4 These statistics can be found at http://pewforum.org/docs/
index.php?DocID=153.

Chapter One

1 A. M. W. Stirling: *The Ways of Yesterday: Being Chronicles of
the Way Family, 1307–1885* (London, 1930), pp.90–7.

2 H. W. L. Way, *History of the Way Family* (privately
published, London, 1914), p.58.

3 Stirling, *The Ways of Yesterday*, p.102.

4 *Leeds Mercury*, 22 September, 1804.

5 On the Parminter sisters and *A la Ronde* see K. Bagshaw, 'Parminter, Jane (1750–1811)', *Oxford Dictionary of National Biography* (Oxford, 2004); H. Mellor, *A La Ronde,* Devon (National Trust Guide, 1991, 1997); D. R. Barber, *A Short History of the Mary Parminter Charity Known as the Point in View Trust* (Plymouth, 1935). The verse is in Stirling, *The Ways of Yesterday,* p.128.

Chapter Two

1 On Evangelicalism, see D. W. Bebbington: *Evangelicalism in Modern Britain: a History from the 1730s to the 1980s* (London, 1989); W. R. Ward, *The Protestant Evangelical Awakening* (Cambridge, 1992); B. Hilton: *The Age of Atonement: the Influence of Evangelicalism on Social and Economic Thought, 1795–1865* (Oxford, 1988) and J. Wolffe, *The Expansion of Evangelicalism: The Age of Wilberforce, More, Chalmers and Finney* (Downers Grove, Illinois, 2007). On John Wesley see J. Kent, *Wesley and the Wesleyans* (Cambridge 2002) and S. Tomkins, *John Wesley: a Biography* (Oxford, 2003); on Charles Simeon see H. E. Hopkins, *Charles Simeon of Cambridge* (London, 1977); the most recent biography of Wilberforce is W. Hague, *William Wilberforce: The Life of the Great Anti-Slavery Campaigner* (London, 2007)

2 Bebbington, *Evangelicalism*, pp.105–8; see also D. Hempton, *The Religion of the People: Methodism and Popular Religion, c.1750–1900* (London, 1996) and F. Baker, *John Wesley and the Church of England* (London, 1970). On the impact of Evangelicalism, se I. Bradley, *The Call to Seriousness: The Evangelical Impact on the Victorians* (London, 1976).

3 On the Clapham Sect see M. M. Hennell, *John Venn and the Clapham Sect* (London, 1958) and S. Tomkins, *The Clapham Sect: How Wilberforce's Circle Changed Britain* (Oxford,

2010). On its role in abolishing the slave trade see J. Walvin, *England, Slaves and Freedom, 1776–1838* (London, 1986) and A. Hochschild, *Bury the Chains: The British Struggle to Abolish Slavery* (London, 2005).

4 Millenarianism has such a long history that a comprehensive bibliography is impossible here: a classic study of medieval millenarianism is N. Cohn, *The Pursuit of the Millennium: Revolutionary Millenarians and Mystical Anarchists of the Middle Ages* (London, 1957), while important analyses of the phenomenon in more recent periods are J. F. C. Harrison, *The Second Coming: Popular Millenarianism, 1780–1850* (London, 1979) and J. Boyer, *When Time Shall Be No More: Prophecy Belief in Modern American Culture* (Cambridge, Mass., 1992).

5 F. Ley, *Mme de Krüdener et son Temps, 1764–1824* (Paris, 1961), p.298.

6 On Joanna Southcott see J. K. Hopkins, *A Woman to Deliver Her People: Joanna Southcott and English Millenarianism in an Era of Revolution* (Austin, Texas, 1982). On millenarianism on both sides of the Channel at this time, see C. Garrett, *Respectable Folly: Millenarianism in the French Revolution in France and England* (Baltimore, 1975).

7 On William Blake and his beliefs see H. Bloom, *Blake's Apocalypse: A Study in Poetic Argument* (London, 1963); P. Ackroyd, *Blake* (London, 1995), and C. Rowlands, *Blake and the Bible* (New Haven and London, 2010). On Richard brothers see C. Roth, *The Nephew of the Almighty: An Experimental Account of the Life and Aftermath of Richard Brothers, RN* (London, 1933).

8 A. M. W. Stirling, *The Ways of Yesterday: Being Chronicles of the Way Family, 1307–1885* (London, 1930), pp.15–21.

9 For publications on the return of the Jews to Palestine, see V. Clark, *Allies for Armageddon: The Rise of Christian Zionism* (New Haven and London, 2007), p.56. For Napoleon and the Jews during the Egyptian campaign see

S. Sebag-Montefiore, *Jerusalem: The Biography* (London, 2011), pp.316–17; see also P. Strathern, *Napoleon in Egypt: The Greatest Glory* (London, 2007).

10 Rev. W. T. Gidney, *The History of the London Society for Promoting Christianity amongst the Jews, from 1809 to 1908* (London, 1908), p.41.

11 For the history of the Jews in Britain see T. M. Endelmann, *The Jews of Britain, 1656–2000* (Berkeley, Los Angeles and London, 2002) and C. Roth, *A History of the Jews in England* (Oxford, 1941).

12 R. Fulford, *Royal Dukes: the Father and Uncles of Queen Victoria* (London, 1933); revised edition 1973, p.287.

13 Gidney, *The History of the London Society,* p.35.

14 Speech of Rev. Legh Richmond in Aid of the London Society, 11 Nov. 1812, *The Jewish Expositor*, Feb. 1813 issue, 1813 volume.

15 H. H. Norris, *The Origins, Progress and existing Circum-stances of the London Society for promoting Christianity among the Jews* (London, 1825), pp.51–2, 146–7, 93; *The Jewish Repository*, May 1813 issue, 1813 volume.
V. Clark, *Allies for Armageddon: The Rise of Christian*

16 *Zionism* (New Haven and London, 2007), p.65.
Stirling, *The Ways of Yesterday*, pp.133–4.

17 Ibid, p.138.

18 G. O. Trevelyan, *Life and Letters of Lord Macaulay* (2 vols,

19 London, 1876), vol.2, p.54. Herbert Marsh, Bishop of Peterborough (1757–1839) was an eminent biblical critic, and High Church oppenent of the interdenominational Bible Society in the Bible Society controversy of 1811–12. Robert Coates (1772–1848) was the wealthy son of a West India merchant and keen amateur actor, with a habit of hiring fashionable theatres for his own, etremely poor, stage performances. Henry Grey Bennet (1777–1836) was a politician and penal reformer.

20 Stirling, *The Ways of Yesterday*, pp.138–9, 141–2.

Chapter Three

1 For such a major figure, Alexander I has been neglected by historians; the most important biography remains N. K. Shil'der, *Imperator Aleksandr I: ego zhizn' i tsarstvovanie (The Emperor Alexander I: his Life and Reign)* (4 vols, St Petersburg, 1897–8). Grand Duke Nikolai Mikhailovich, *L'Empereur Alexandre Ier: Essai d'Etude Historique* (2 vols, St Petersburg, 1912) is also significant. There are two modern popular biographies: A. Palmer, *Alexander I: Tsar of War and Peace* (London, 1974), and H. Troyat, *Alexandre Ier: le Sphinx du Nord* (Paris, 1980; English translation by J. Pinkham as *Alexander of Russia: Napoleon's Conqueror*, London, 1984). There is also a good short study, J. M. Hartley, *Alexander I* (London, 1994).

2 On the Jewish Statute of 1804 see J. D. Klier, *Russia Gathers her Jews: The Origins of the 'Jewish Question' in Russia, 1772–1825* (DeKalb, Illinois, 1986), pp.116–43.

3 F. Ley, *Alexandre 1er et sa Sainte-Alliance (1811–1825), avec des documents inédits* (Paris, 1975), pp.52–3.

4 F. Ley, *Mme de Krüdener et son temps, 1764–1824* (Paris, 1961), p.298; Hartley, *Alexander I*, pp.116–17.

5 The best biography of Mme von Krüdener is Ley, *Mme de Krüdener*, which draws on important archives in private hands. On Golitsyn as Alexander's confidant, see Grand Duke Nikolai Mikhailovich, *L'Empereur Alexandre Ier,* vol.1, p.173.

6 For Castlereagh's attitude see J. W. Derry, *Castlereagh* (London, 1976), pp.186–8; for the argument that the alliance was a hypocritical ploy see, among others, H.-H. Pirenne, *La Sainte-Alliance:Organisation Européene de la Paix Mondiale* (2 vols, Neuchatel, 1946–9).

7 F. Ley, *Alexandre Ier et sa Sainte-Alliance* (Paris, 1975), p.217.

8 Ibid, p.176.

9 Rev. R. Pinkerton to Rev. Dr Steinkopff, 20 April (old style)

1817, published in *A Letter Addressed to the Right Reverend the Bishop of St David's, Joint Patron of the London Society for Promoting Christianity among the Jews, by the Rev Lewis Way, MA* (second edition, Dublin and London, 1820), p.63.

10 Rev. W. T. Gidney, *The History of the London Society for Promoting Christianity amongst the Jews, from 1809 to 1908* (London, 1908), p.58.

11 A. M. W. Stirling, *The Ways of Yesterday, Being chronicles of the Way family, 1307–1885* (London, 1830), pp.151–4.

12 Ibid., p.156.

Chapter Four

1 D. J. Goldberg and J. D. Rayner, *The Jewish People: Their History and Their Religion* (London, 1987), 1989 edition, pp.132–3. Important modern works that cover the Jews in Europe in this period are D. Vital, *A People Apart: The Jews in Europe, 1789–1939* (Oxford, 1999); A. Elon, *The Pity of it all: A History of the Jews in Germany, 1743–1933* (London, 2002); A. Eisenbach, *The Emancipation of the Jews in Poland, 1780–1870* (Oxford, 1991); J. D. Klier, *Russia Gathers her Jews: The Origins of the 'Jewish Question' in Russia, 1772–1825* (DeKalb, Ill., 1986); H. M. Sachar, *The Course of Modern Jewish History* (New York, 1958, 1977).

2 Sachar, *The Course of Modern Jewish History* (1977 edition), p.66.

3 Vital, *A People Apart,* pp.61–2; Sachar, *The Course of Modern Jewish History,* pp.100–3.

4 L. Way, *Mémoires sur l'Etat des Israélites, Dédiés et Présentés à Leurs Majestés Impériales et Royales, Réunies au Congrès d'Aix-la-Chapelle* (Paris, 1819), p.63 (authors' translation).

5 *A Letter Addressed to the Right Reverend the Lord Bishop of St David's, Joint Patron of the London Society for Promoting Christianity among the Jews, by the Rev Lewis Way, MA* (Second edition, Dublin and London, 1820), p.31.

6 Ibid., p.19; *The Jewish Expositor, and Friend of Israel* (16 vols, London, 1816–31), vol.3 (1818), p.152.

7 *A Letter to the Bishop of St David's*, p.27.

8 On George Rose, see C. A. Harris, 'Rose, George Henry (1770–1855)' rev. H. C .G. Matthew, *Oxford Dictionary of National Biography* (Oxford, 2004); Lewis to Mary Way, 'Home of Copernicus, Thorn', 14 November 1817, Hartley Library, University of Southampton, Ms 85, Parkes Papers, 29/5/19 (Papers of Lewis Way).

9 Lewis to Mary Way, 8 November 1817, ibid, 29/5/18.

10 *A Letter to the Bishop of St David's*, pp.36–7.

11 Lewis to Elizabeth Way, 'Gulben, half-way between Riga and St Petersburg', 7 December 1817, Hartley Library, Ms 85, Parkes Papers, 29/5/25.

12 A. M. W. Stirling, *The Ways of Yesterday, being chronicles of the Way family, 1307–1885* (London, 1930), p.168.

13 Ibid., pp.169-70.

14 Ibid., p.70.

Chapter Five

1 Lewis Way, 'Memorandum of Interview with His Imperial Majesty Alexander, Emperor of all the Russias', private collection, p.4.

2 A. M. W. Stirling, *The Ways of Yesterday: Being Chronicles of the Way Family, 1307–1885* (London, 1930), pp.172–3.

3 *Thomas Clarkson's Interview with the Emperor Alexander I of Russia, at Aix-la-Chapelle, as Told by Himself* (Wisbech, 1930), p.20.

4 Hartley Library, University of Southampton, Ms 85, Parkes Papers, 29/4/1, p.8 (Papers of Lewis Way).

5 Stirling, *The Ways of Yesterday*, p.175.

6 Way, 'Memorandum of Interview', private collection, p.13.

7 Stirling, *The Ways of Yesterday*, p.178

8 F. Ley, *Alexandre Ier et sa Sainte-Alliance (1811–1825), avec des documents inédits* (Paris, 1975), p.195.

9 Ibid., p.241; Stirling, *The Ways of Yesterday*, p.148.

10 P. W. Schroeder, *The Transformation of European Politics,1763-1848* (Oxford, 1994), pp.587–8, 617–21.

11 Cited in J.-H. Pirenne, *La Sainte-Alliance: Organisation Européenne de la Paix Mondiale* (2 vols, Neuchatel, 1946–9), vol.2, p.87.

12 Cited in Ley, *Alexandre Ier*, p.198.

13 Stirling, *The Ways of Yesterday*, pp.174–5.

14 *Thoughts on the Scriptural Expectations of the Christian Church, by Basilicus* (reprinted from *The Jewish Expositor*, Gloucester, 1823), pp.106–7.

15 *The Jewish Expositor, and Friend of Israel* (16 vols, London, 1816–31), 1818 volume, July 1818 issue, p.278.

16 Ibid., p.277.

17 Stirling, *The Ways of Yesterday*, p.182.

18 Hartley Library, Ms 85, Parkes Papers, 29/4/1, p.8; Stirling, *The Ways of Yesterday*, p.184.

19 Hartley Library, Ms 85, Parkes Papers, 29/4/1, p.75; Stirling, *The Ways of Yesterday*, pp.184–5.

20 Ibid., pp.186–7.

21 Ibid., p.190.

22 Ibid., p.193.

23 Ibid.

24 *Mémoires sur l'Etat des Israélites, Dédiés et présentés à Leurs Majestés Impériales et Royales,Réunies au Congrès d'Aix-la-Chapelle* (Paris, 1819), pp.25–6.

25 Ibid., p.69.

26 Stirling, *The Ways of Yesterday*, p.195.

27 Ibid., p.196; *Mémoires sur l'Etat des Israélites*, pp.21–2, 24.

28 Ibid., p.79.

29 Stirling, *The Ways of Yesterday*, p.197.

30 *Mémoire sur L'Etat des Israélites*, p.29.

31 Hartley Library, Ms 85, Parkes Papers, 29/4/1, pp.77–8.

32 Stirling, *The Ways of Yesterday*, p.198.

Chapter Six

1 A. M. W. Stirling, *The Ways of Yesterday: Being Chronicles of the Way Family, 1307–1885* (London, 1930), pp.305–6.

2 Earl of Bessborough, *A Place in the Forest: Being the Story of Stansted in Sussex* (London, 1958), p.81; Robert Gittings, *John Keats* (London, 1968), pp.283–8.

3 *Reminiscences of Mrs Finn, Member of the Royal Asiatic Society* (London, 1929), p.19.

4 For McCaul see W. A. J. Archbold, 'McCaul, Alexander (1799–1863), Rev. H. C. G. Matthew, *Oxford Dictionary of National Biography* (Oxford, 2004).

5 On these European developments, see P. W. Schroeder, *The Transformation of European Politics, 1763–1848* (Oxford, 1994), pp.591–614, and F. Ley, *Alexandre Ier et sa Sainte-Alliance* (Paris, 1975), pp.228–36.

6 On Henry Handley Norris, see P. B. Nockles, 'Norris, Henry Handley (1771–1850)', *ODNB*. Norris was the leader of a powerful High Church and anti-Evangelical faction within the Church of England known as the 'Hackney Phalanx', and had such influence with the prime minister Lord Liverpool that he was known as 'the Bishop-maker'. It seems likely that it was Norris's use of these connections that ensured Stansted did not get its charter. Norris's attack on the London Society, which was vitriolic and ran to 500 pages, was published as *The Origins, Progress and Existing Circumstances of the London Society for Promoting Christianity among the Jews* (London, 1825). Significantly, the most forthright statement on record that the Duke of Kent withdrew his patronage of the Society because of unease at its proselytising methods comes here, p.93.

7 Stirling, *The Ways of Yesterday*, p.225.

8 Bessborough, *A Place in the Forest*, p.75.

9 Stirling, *The Ways of Yesterday*, p.229.

10 Ibid., p.232.

11 Ibid., p.233.

12 On Lady Hester Stanhope see C. L. Meryon, *Memoirs of the Lady Hester Stanhope as Related by Herself in Conversation with her Physician: Comprising her Opinions and Anecdotes of some of the most remarkable Persons of her Time* (3 vols, London, 1845) and *The Travels of the Lady Hester Stanhope forming the Completion of her Memoirs, as Narrated by her Physician* (3 vols, London, 1846), J. Haslip, *Lady Hester Stanhope* (1934) and L. Gibb, *Lady Hester: Queen of the East* (London, 2005).

13 See Gibb, *Lady Hester*, pp.89–91, 160–1.

14 Stirling, *The Ways of Yesterday,* p.249.

15 Ibid., pp.247–8.

16 Meryon, *Memoirs of the Lady Hester Stanhope*, vol.1, pp.134–7.

17 Stirling, *The Ways of Yesterday*, p.259.

18 *Thoughts on the Scriptural Expectations of the Christian Church, by Basilicus* (reprinted from *The Jewish Expositor,* Gloucester, 1823), p.101.

19 Stirling, *The Ways of Yesterday*, p.268.

20 Ibid., p.271.

21 Ibid., p.275.

22 Ibid., pp.275–7.

23 Ibid., pp.279–80.

24 On Dr Jephson see E. G. Baxter, *Dr Jephson of Leamington Spa*, ed. J. Lane and R. Bearman (Leamington Spa, 1980).

25 Stirling, *The Ways of Yesterday*, p.282.

26 There is a memorial to Way inside the church; his actual tomb is below in its vault.

27 Stirling, *The Ways of Yesterday*, p.288.

28 Rev. W. T. Gidney, *The History of the London Society for Promoting Christianity amongst the Jews, from 1809 to 1908* (London, 1908), pp.416–17.

Epilogue

1 Shaftesbury authorised a biography during his lifetime, which appeared just after his death: E. Hodder, *The Life and Work of the Seventh Earl of Shaftesbury, KG* (3 vols, London, 1886). The edition used here is the 'popular edition' of 1887. Modern scholarly biographies are G. B. A. M. Finlayson, *The Seventh Earl of Shaftesbury, 1801–1885* (London, 1981) and J. Pollock, *Shaftesbury: The Poor Man's Earl* (London, 1985).

2 Finlayson, *Shaftesbury,* p.113.

3 J. Frankel, *The Damascus Affair: 'Ritual Murder', Politics and the Jews in 1840* (Cambridge, 1997), p.392.

4 W. A. J. Archbold, 'McCaul, Alexander (1799–1863)', Rev. H. C. G. Matthew, *Oxford Dictionary of National Biography* (Oxford, 2004); Finlayson, *Shaftesbury*, pp.154–5.

5 Finlayson, *Shaftesbury*, p.113.

6 See P. W. Schroeder, *The Transformation of European Politics, 1763–1848* (Oxford, 1994), pp.736–56.

7 Shaftesbury, diary entry for 1 August 1840, cited in Hodder, *The Seventh Earl of Shaftesbury*, p.167.

8 Frankel, *The Damascus Affair*, p.307.

9 V. Clark, *Allies for Armageddon: The Rise of Christian Zionism* (New Haven and London, 2007), p.72.

10 P. R. Wilkinson, *For Zion's Sake: Christian Zionism and the Role of John Nelson Darby* (Milton Keynes, 2007), p.218.

11 Clark, *Allies for Armageddon*, pp.98–100.

12 Wilkinson, *For Zion's Sake*, pp.218–19.

13 D. Stewart, *Theodor Herzl, Artist and Politician* (London, 1974), pp.271–2.

14 Ibid., p.336.

15 Wilkinson, *For Zion's Sake*, p.220; Clark, *Allies for Armageddon,* p.108.

16 Weizmann wrote his autobiography, *Trial and Error: The Autobiography of Chaim Weizmann* (London, 1949); the best modern biography is N. Rose, *Chaim Weizmann* (New York and London, 1986). On his relations with Balfour, and on

the Balfour Declaration, there are two recent works: G. Lewis, *Balfour and Weizmann: The Zionist, the Zealot and the Emergence of Israel* (London, 2009) and J. Schneer, *The Balfour Declaration: The Origins of the Arab-Israeli Conflict* (London, 2010).

17 Weizmann, *Trial and Error*, p.194; B. Tuchman, *Bible and Sword: How the British came to Palestine* (New York, 1956; edition used here London, 1982), p.83.

18 B. E. C. Dugdale, *Arthur James Balfour, First Earl Balfour* (2 vols, London, 1936), vol.1, p.433; Tuchman, *Bible and Sword*, p.311.

19 Wilkinson, *For Zion's Sake*, p.221.

20 Clark, *Allies for Armageddon*, p.58.

21 See T. C. F. Stunt, 'Darby, John Nelson (1800–1882)', *ODNB*; *Letters of John Nelson Darby* (3 vols, London, 1886–89); Clark, *Allies for Armageddon*, pp 61–3, 80–6.

22 *Letters of John Nelson Darby,* vol. 1, p.7.

23 Clark, *Allies for Armageddon*, p.63.

24 Ibid., pp.63, 86–92.

25 S. Spector, *Evangelicals and Israel: the Story of American Christian Zionism* (Oxford, 2009), p.27; Clark, *Allies for Armageddon*, p.144.

26 Ibid., p.187.

27 Princeton Religion Research Report, 2002: 'Describing Self as Born-Again or Evangelical', bar graph, online, http://wheaton.edu/isae/Gallup-Bar-graph.html.

28 Clark, *Allies for Armageddon*, pp.193–4.

29 Jerry Falwell speaking on 'Sixty Minutes' CBS news programme, 10 December 2003.